The Humanities: An Appraisal

This Volume is Published in Celebration of the
HUNDREDTH ANNIVERSARY
of the Founding of the University of Wisconsin

—————THE CONTRIBUTORS

Cleanth Brooks
Philo M. Buck
Serge Chermayeff
Donald J. Grout
Henry Guerlac
Howard Mumford Jones
Rudolf Kolisch
Clark G. Kuebler
Howard Lee Nostrand
Nathan M. Pusey
Wolfgang Stechow
Eliseo Vivas

THE

HUMANITIES

An Appraisal

Edited by Julian Harris

THE UNIVERSITY OF WISCONSIN PRESS

Madison, 1962

Publisher's Note

For bibliographical reasons, Professor Julian Harris, chairman of the committee responsible for this book, has been designated editor. Listing volumes of essays written under separate authorship presents problems to bibliographers which do not easily lend themselves to practical solution. The Press, therefore, feels that scholars will be grateful for a simple entry under which this book may appear in files, catalogues, and bibliographies.

Introduction

Within the last three or four years, a number of symposia on the humanities have been held in this country, and others are being projected. Books and many papers on the subject are continually being published. Therefore it occurs to me that the public may well wonder why such meetings are held and why the papers should be brought out in book form. Of course when a symposium on enzymes or on nuclear fission is announced, everyone knows at once that its purpose is to bring together the specialists who can add to the sum total of knowledge on the subject; and everyone also knows that the papers will be comprehensible and significant to only a relatively small group of scientists. But neither the *raison d'être* nor the clientele of a symposium on the humanities is so clear-cut.

In planning the symposium on the Humanities in American Society, the Executive Committee of the Division of Humanities hoped not so much to add to our knowledge of the role or function of the humanistic studies as to call to the attention of the larger public the existence of the humanities and, so to speak, to present them in action. In order to give due importance to the fine arts and music the meetings were scheduled to coincide with the exhibition of masterpieces from the Metropolitan Museum at the University of Wisconsin, and the final session of the

symposium was devoted to a concert of chamber music
by the Pro Arte Quartet. Round tables were organized
for the discussion of music and the fine arts as humanistic
studies. Moreover, we attempted to find subjects of general interest for the longer papers and especially to avoid
such subjects as "What is wrong with the humanities?"
or "The enduring values of the humanities." After all,
their merits and their shortcomings—particularly the latter—have been frequently discussed, both by the humanists themselves, who by nature and training are given
to self-analysis and self-criticism, and by their opponents,
who seem bent on replacing intellectual formation, the
traditional objective of the Liberal Arts College, with
a sort of rudimentary, standardized, and integrated indoctrination about democratic society.

However, although the symposium was in no sense
intended as a defense of the humanities, the committee
hoped from the beginning that it would cause the public
to give some thought to the significance of the humanistic
disciplines and to their importance in the education of
future citizens. For many people have a vague impression
that the humanities are old-fashioned or even reactionary
and that most college students devote their time largely
to this part of the curriculum. This impression persists
in spite of the "flight from the humanities" which has
been going on for at least the last fifty years and in spite
of the fact that the humanistic studies have come to
play a pitifully small part in the education of the average
high school and college student. In order to make way
for science and the social studies, we have reduced the
humanistic content of the curriculum to the point where
the great works of foreign literature have disappeared

from the classroom—at least so far as the great mass of students is concerned. This is extremely unfortunate, because classics such as the works of Plato, Montaigne, Rousseau, and many others are basically as new as any modern writers on politics or society—and perhaps more challenging to the adult mind. It should be obvious that literature, which is after all the richest of the social studies, is indispensable. In fact, before the modern social scientists worked out the regrettable professional jargon currently used in their writings, all the important works in that field *were* literature.

Meanwhile, with the publication of numerous curriculum committee reports, the introduction of "humanities" courses in certain colleges, and the extension of the "great books" movement, people may well begin to believe that the colleges have finally abandoned the elective system, which obviously places too much confidence in the wisdom of young and inexperienced students, and that we are now giving a truly liberal education to all young Americans. But this impression would be equally untrue and also unfortunate. For even if we assume that these new curricula are perfect in every way—and no one would make such a boast—there are at least three reasons why they cannot be counted upon to produce such a happy result: (1) in practically all cases, they apply only to the first two years of college and, consequently, have no bearing upon the four to six years of high school training, which is geared to mass education, nor upon the last two years of college, which for the great majority of students are devoted almost exclusively to specialization in science, social science, engineering, commerce, advertising, or what not; (2) the great majority of colleges, junior colleges, and normal schools, in setting up the so-called new curricula, have merely reshuffled the elective system and rechristened a few courses; and (3) in the few institutions in which a really new and presumably improved curriculum *has* been introduced, the old and presumably unimproved curricula usually remain as rivals, very successful rivals from the point of view of popularity. Consequently it is clear that an insignificant proportion of students is deriving much benefit from the new curricula and, therefore, it would be wishful thinking to assume that the average young American is getting a substantially richer intellectual diet than the college generations of ten, twenty, or thirty years ago. It is sincerely to be hoped that a superior curriculum will come out of the fine educational ferment we are experiencing; but it is only fair to remark that uncontrolled fermentation is perhaps as likely to result in vinegar as in fine wine.

This is not the moment to pronounce a new jeremiad about the low state of literacy of the average college graduate, for the public has been reminded frequently enough that the selective-service dragnet turned up many high school and even college graduates who were "functionally illiterate." But since observers are continually harping on the fact that most adult Americans never read anything other than the comic strips, advertisements, headlines, sport news, gossip columns, cheap fiction, and mystery stories, perhaps a brief editorial comment on this point would be permissible. The reading habits of the population suggest either that our system of education does not give students enough experience in reading good books to develop good taste in reading matter or else that it does not give them sufficient skill in reading for them to be able to read good books without outside aid or compulsion. It is no doubt true that many people feel neither the desire nor the need for richer intellectual and artistic experience; but on the other hand, it is equally certain that a great many people *do* feel a very real need and indeed an intense longing for the things from which fate (or short-sighted educators) has turned them aside in their formative years. This yearning is reflected both by the popularity of adult education, the book clubs, and the "great books" movement and by the large memberships in symphony societies and art associations all over the country. But purchasing great books, in five-foot lots or in smaller parcels, is a futile gesture if the purchaser has not learned during his formative years to read and appreciate good books. And many of the people who go through the motions of going to symphony concerts and art galleries in the hope of experiencing vicariously some sort of aesthetic emotion are doomed to frustration and disappointment because they have never been given even an elementary understanding of music and the fine arts. Many college-bred people who would like nothing better than to devote a part of their leisure to the pursuit of serious reading and the arts find that they must resign themselves to the easier joys of sporting events, the cinema, radio, and even television. They find, too late, that the enjoyment of literature cannot be had in exchange for money. It is the fault of the colleges and high schools that they do not make young people understand that our priceless cultural heritage is valueless except to those who are willing to devote serious and prolonged personal effort to taking possession of it.

Therefore it may be permissible, finally, for me to urge

the readers of this book to try to persuade a few members of the rising generations that education is, first and foremost, the development of the intellectual and moral faculties, and that they can develop these faculties only by using them. André Gide has said that each man must create his own soul. Even if this remark is taken as a sort of figure of speech, it suggests in a striking way that a soul (or mind) which is carefully nurtured and exercised, which is furnished with a rich store of ideas and a firsthand acquaintance with the great minds of art and literature, and which has been given the habit of pondering important things deeply makes its possessor a more mature individual and also a more useful member of society than the "untrammeled soul" which does nothing while the physical man devotes his life to getting and spending.

If the reader wonders why _he_ is asked to act as adviser to high school and college students, the reason is that, generally speaking, as things stand at present, the future members of the intellectual aristocracy are simply not receiving a diet which is worthy of them nor one which is capable of developing their intellectual powers to the fullest. It is right and proper, certainly, that our system of education should supply the needs of the majority, and it is inevitable that it should continue to yield to the pressure for more and more vocational training. Therefore we can expect neither the high schools nor the colleges to oppose the trend successfully. Besides, many school men, and, indeed, college professors, believe very sincerely that "it makes no difference _what_ you study," that "mental discipline is a meaningless expression," that culture is for girls' finishing schools, and that "education in a democracy should be purely practical." With such an educational creed, which consists of negation, confusion, and half-truths, not to say unwitting obscurantism, educators will inevitably leave the education of young Americans in their own hands at a time when they are in no position to make Spartan decisions. But Spartan decisions must be made if the best minds are to attain their fullest development; we cannot afford to leave the training of our best minds largely to the caprice of young—and consequently ignorant—students. Therefore, since the schools and colleges are content, by and large, to supply the kind of training which is demanded, it is apparently up to the enlightened public to see to it that there is a greater demand for humanistic study.

If, then, after giving the matter serious thought, the reader of this volume is convinced that students cannot become liberally educated without serious and prolonged study of languages and literature, of history, philosophy, mathematics, music, and the fine arts, it is his solemn duty to see to it that at least a few promising members of his community undertake to devote a serious amount of time and effort to such work *throughout their high school and college training*. Rousseau said that democracy is an ideal form of government which can be effective only in a society of gods. Without aiming so high, we might at least try to raise somewhat the level of literacy, personal culture, and intellectual formation of our college graduates; for we shall have to produce a vastly increased number of people whose intellectual and moral faculties are developed to the utmost if, in spite of ever increasing pressure, both from the right and from the left, democracy is to be preserved, cherished, or even understood.

The members of the Executive Committee of the Division of Humanities which sponsored the symposium are: Einar I. Haugen, Professor of Scandinavian Languages; R-M. S. Heffner, Professor of German; Rudolph E. Langer, Professor of Mathematics; Paul L. MacKendrick, Associate Professor of Classics; Gaines Post, Professor of History; Ricardo Quintana, Professor of English; Samuel Rogers, Professor of French; Robert C. Stauffer, Assistant Professor of History of Science; and Edmund I. Zawacki, Associate Professor of Slavic Languages. Although I cannot certify that every member of the committee would subscribe in detail to the above paragraphs, at least I can say that I have discussed with them more than once the function of the humanities and that they would agree in principle with the views expressed. I should like to extend to them my personal thanks and those of the faculty of the Division of Humanities for their contribution to the success of the symposium. I hope very much that the fine rapport which grew up among the members of the committee in the course of the meetings devoted to working out the details of the program will continue to exist and that it will be a means of strengthening the ideals of humanistic study in the University of Wisconsin.

The names of the guest speakers whose papers are published below are alone enough to guarantee the value and the success of the volume. Most of them came to Madison from a considerable distance and at great personal sacrifice; and moreover while here they gave generously of their time for both public discussion and private conversation. The fact that they interrupted their teaching, writing, and administrative duties in the middle of a week and in the middle of an academic term is ample testimony to the importance they attach to the humanities in American society. The University of Wisconsin is deeply grateful to them both for the brilliance and charm of their individual papers and discussions and for the total impression made by the symposium upon the university community. Their visit to Madison will not soon be forgotten.

J. H.

Madison, Wisconsin
October, 1949

Contents

The Humanities: An Appraisal

1 The Quick and the Dead
A Comment on Humanistic Studies

Cleanth Brooks

T HE late poet, William Butler Yeats, provided for his curious and at points wrong-headed *Oxford Book of Modern Verse* a very brilliant introduction. He writes there: "When my generation denounced scientific humanitarian pre-occupation, psychological curiosity, rhetoric, we had not found what ailed Victorian literature. The Elizabethans had all these things, especially rhetoric." What then did ail Victorian literature? What is Yeats's diagnosis? "The mischief began," Yeats declares, "the mischief began at the end of the seventeenth century when man became passive before a mechanized nature. . . ." It is a brilliant insight and I think a true one. It can be illuminating even for those who reject Yeats's conviction that Victorian literature quite obviously suffered from some dire ailment. But Yeats does not insist upon his specific dating of the onset of the malady. He goes on to write: "Or I may dismiss all that ancient history and say [the mischief] began when Stendhal described a masterpiece as a 'mirror dawdling down a lane.' "

Yeats's own career as a poet, as we know, shows the mirror discarded for the lamp. But I do not propose to discuss here either Yeats's poetry or his theory of what happened to English literature from the seventeenth century to our day. Rather I propose to use his comment for a discussion of the humanities. And I begin, like Yeats, by assuming that something ails them, that someone has played the devil somewhere, that the mischief at some time *did* begin. Like Yeats again, I am not so much concerned with just when the mischief began—with the importation of German seminar methods, say—as with defining the mischief. And I shall define it in a paraphrase of Yeats's terms, thus: "The mischief began when the scholar became passive before literature conceived as mere mechanism; when, taking the poem to be a mirror, the scholar examined it as a mere reflection of the world rather than the re-creation of a world."

Thus we get, on the part of the literary scholar, the sociology of the mirror, the counting and cataloguing of the exhibits there portrayed. In an amusing passage of his essay, Yeats describes an extreme of the poet's "passivity" in writing that some poets have gone so far as to withdraw into the quicksilver at the back of the mirror, that is to say, the creative intelligence becomes absorbed into, and merged with, the reflecting instrument itself. But even here, I think, my parallel with scholarship holds, for the scholars have gone on to give us every sort of analysis of the mirror from dissertations on optics to elaborate chemical analyses of the glass out of which the mirror is made, or of the quicksilver which backs it. Indeed, the literary scholar's labors have been strenuous and methodical. But too often they have been merely mechanical and, being mechanical, have missed what literature has to give.

One of my colleagues, who teaches political science, introduced me to a useful term in his profession. Certain studies in political science, it seems, are called "manhole-cover-counting" studies. In literary scholarship we do not count manhole covers, but we sometimes count commas, or verbal parallels, or "influences." That is our particular way of treating the literary document as inert—of becoming passive before the poem as a mechanical thing.

I am glad that Yeats refused to find the ailment of Victorian literature in its "scientific humanitarian pre-occupation" or in its "psychological curiosity." These interests do not in themselves harm literature; they may be healthy. This observation applies not only to literature but also to the study of literature. Our preoccupation with scientific humanitarianism has certainly carried us to some extremes. It has warped our judgment of certain works, causing us to undervalue certain novels because they do not contain sufficiently buoyant messages for a democratic culture, and to overvalue others because we think that they do. By the same token, our psychological curiosity has allowed us to devote vast study to the author's motives and psychic disturbances, and sometimes to read works of art merely for their interest as case histories. Even so, our scientific humanitarian preoccupation and our psychological curiosity are normal and to be expected, and are in themselves good. I should like to make it very plain that I am not attacking either as such. Nor am I making here the obvious and easy attack upon our characteristic literary studies as conscious studies, and because conscious, therefore pedantic. Literary study, like any other, necessarily involves careful analysis of one sort or another. It may involve methodical operations. We may need to count the commas, or collate editions, to catalogue variants or to work out etymologies. In suggesting that the scholar of the humanities ought to reject mechanism, I am not urging that he cease to be a scholar. A great deal of drudgery is always necessary and work that entails it may be significant and important.

I want to recur, at this point, to the Yeats analogy. The mechanized nature before which the poet became passive was, of course, a nature whose throat had been cut by Descartes. As you see, I am revising somewhat—as I take it Yeats would revise—the terms of the well-known indictment. For properly speaking, Descartes did not cut the throat of poetry. It was nature that he reduced to a mechanism before which the poet, in Yeats's terms, became passive. This passive poet's characteristic task becomes that of dressing up with emotional qualities which are inside him, and therefore private and subjective, a nature which is outside him and abstract. In this process, the scientist gains a world that he can describe in abstract notation; the poet wins a kingdom of the emotions within, which he can rule despotically, but his kingdom has the unreality of the enchanted castle of the fairy tale, or of Tennyson's palace of art. In this process it is the creative imagination that loses its creative power. It atrophies into the passive mirror—the imagination as a reflecting instrument. The temptation to see the poem as a body of fact dressed in a garb of rhetoric has been almost irresistible.

If the poet acquiesced in the cutting of the throat of poetry, the literary scholar too often in his turn has played the role of the dissector and the embalmer. He has been concerned with measuring a lifeless body, and he has been tempted to take over from his scientific brethren techniques admirably adapted to this kind of measurement. But it is the living poetry that interests us. It is living poetry that gives the humanities their value and makes them worthy of preservation; and techniques which are necessary to, and serve accurately for, the measurement of a human being who has become a thing, an object to be treated mechanically, do not work at all well to measure a body which is alive and in characteristic motion.

Now I am pressing my point very hard here, and perhaps unfairly. But I think that the point is of crucial importance and has to be made. Let me suggest an analogy. Madame Tussaud's Wax Works certainly serve a purpose. The wax works do, in a very real sense, re-create the past. Famous and notorious figures are to be seen there in characteristic costume, and they even possess a certain simulation of life. For instance, there is the museum attendant to whom one addresses a question, only to find that one is speaking to one of the exhibits. Yet the study of literature ought not to be merely a tour through a kind of refined Madame Tussaud's. And, with all reverence speaking, the study of literature is too often merely such a tour, with the professor himself the only live figure among the exhibits, and sometimes, yielding to the morgue-like atmosphere, actually becoming himself only a livelier-looking wax effigy.

In so far as we study the literature of the past merely as a record of past customs, past habits, past manners, past fashions in taste, it is proper that it be treated as a kind of museum. And let me add that such study has its uses. I am in favor of museums. I myself dote upon them. And the museum attendant has a necessary and thoroughly honorable function. But if our interest in the literature of the past is merely an interest in it as history, then the large claims made for the humanities in the past as furnishing a living discipline had better be withdrawn. And we who teach the humanities ought to be prepared to assume a much more modest and more humble place, an honorable corner, say, in the lobby of the history department, but a small corner; for that is as much as I think we deserve.

If, on the other hand, the teaching of literature does involve an active discipline; does promise to form and regenerate taste; does propose to balance our society's emphasis on machinery and techniques with a powerful counteremphasis on ends and values, then I think we must admit that by and large we have failed rather sensationally.

We have not supplied that counteremphasis on ends and values. We have let popular taste get almost completely out of hand: witness the state of the popular, mass-produced arts. And one cause of our failure, I am convinced, lies in the inapplicability of the methods that we characteristically use and our misconception of what acceptable methods are.

I hope that you will attend carefully to what I shall say at this point. In the first place, I certainly do not think that our failure needs to be set down solely to our own mistakes, numerous as these are. The general cultural situation is admittedly a most difficult one. In the second place, I do not suggest that there is some one indispensable method guaranteed to produce results. That is simply to replace one piece of mechanism with another, and, as Arnold pointed out, our pervasive error is our reliance on machinery. I say this feelingly, because, much to my own mortification, I am sometimes associated with a fabulous gadget, a kind of combination burglar's jimmy and patent can-opener, guaranteed even in the hands of a child to open up any given poem in twenty-five minutes.

In the third place, my words here can easily be misinterpreted to mean that I hold textual criticism to be foolish; the writing of footnotes, a waste of time; literary history, dull nonsense; and that I suggest that we throw overboard and forthwith the various disciplines of the modern graduate school. I am saying nothing of the kind, for all that I am urging is that we not conceive of our role in terms of these conventional tools. What I am saying is that the literary scholar shall not, to paraphrase Yeats's words, become passive before the poem considered as an inert body. He must realize that it is a living organism, and whatever measurements he needs to make of its substance, he should try also to measure it in its characteristic mode. In short, he must deal with it ultimately as a work of art and not merely as a grammatical or historical or sociological or political or biographical document. Again, please note carefully what I am saying. I would not limit the writer to doing only this, and certainly I am not denying that in order to encompass the work as a work of art he may need to make use of the resources of a half-dozen disciplines—grammar, textual criticism, history, and so forth.

This last point, however, I am afraid you may dismiss as a merely polite assertion, a diplomatic concession to scholarship, and one that does not have to be taken very seriously. And I know of no other way to prevent your making such a discount than by offering a concrete illustration. To provide such an illustration, I should like to read you a sonnet by a rather minor seventeenth-century poet, Sir Richard Fanshawe. Many of you have heard of his translation of *Il Pastor Fido* and some of you have

read it. Sir Herbert Grierson prints the sonnet in his
Oxford Book of Seventeenth Century Verse. It is entitled
"The Fall."

I think that the poem has merit, although it is obviously
not a great poem. At any rate, I hope that it will serve
to illustrate my point that the study of literature as
literature—as art—does not imply any dismissal of our
conventional graduate school disciplines as worthless.

The bloudy trunck of him who did possesse
    Above the rest a haplesse happy state,
    This little Stone doth Seale, but not depresse,
    And scarce can stop the rowling of his fate.

Brasse Tombes which justice hath deny'd t' his fault,
    The common pity to his vertues payes,
    Adorning an Imaginary vault,
    Which from our minds time strives in vaine to raze.

Ten yeares the world upon him falsly smild,
    Sheathing in fawning lookes the deadly knife
    Long aymed at his head; That so beguild
    It more securely might bereave his Life;

    Then threw him to a Scaffold from a Throne.
    Much Doctrine lyes under this little Stone.

Whose is the bloody trunk that has been tossed to a
scaffold from a throne? Grierson's note states that the
poem is "On the death of Charles I." Now the poem was
first printed in the second issue of the first edition of
Il Pastor Fido, the book from which I have just read it,
and that book is dated 1648. Charles was beheaded on
January 30, 1649. But of course we must remember that

at this period the new year began on March 25, and that, therefore, the execution of Charles took place on January 30, 1648, old style. It is possible, therefore, that though the book in which the poem appears is dated 1648, still the poem might have been written after January 30 and set up and printed by March 24. The interval between January 30 and March 25, however, is short, for into it we must crowd not only the composition of the poem but also the printer's composition and presswork.

There is still further evidence of a bibliographical kind against the case for Charles. Fanshawe's translation of *Il Pastor Fido* was printed in 1647 by the widow of Robert Raworth. On the sixth of February, 1648, she assigned to the printer Moseley this translation together with "divers other poems" by Fanshawe. Taken literally, this statement says that our poem, one of those "divers other poems," had been written at least a year before Charles's death. But in any case, the evidence bears hard against the case for Charles. For it seems most unlikely that if Moseley acquired the book early in February, 1648, he waited a year to bring it out—all the more unlikely in view of the fact that he made use of the unsold sheets of the *Pastor Fido* taken over from Raworth, and thus had already in print over two-thirds of the book as he finally issued it.

When we look into the poem itself, the evidence against any reference to Charles accumulates. The poem insists upon the smallness of the stone that marks the victim's grave. "Little stone" is stressed at the beginning of the poem and at the end. This detail ill accords with Charles's burial in the vault of Henry VIII in St. George's, Windsor.

But the ninth line of the poem poses a still greater difficulty. The ninth line reads:

Ten yeares the world upon him falsly smild.

Charles I had reigned some twenty-four years, not ten. And if we try to save Grierson's account by making the ten years refer to a particular period of Charles's reign— the poem makes it plain that it is the last ten years before the fall—the passage becomes nonsense; for Charles's last ten years, filled as they were with his conflict with the Long Parliament, the Civil War, and his imprisonment and trial, are surely the least smiling period of his whole career.

The truth of the matter is that the sonnet has nothing at all to do with the execution of Charles I. It seems to comment upon the fall of Thomas Wentworth, the Earl of Strafford, who was impeached, tried for treason, and beheaded on May 12, 1642. "Ten yeares the world upon him falsly smild" makes perfect sense when applied to Strafford, who was Charles's great coadjutor during most of the eleven years in which the king tried to rule without a parliament. If we must be more specific, he was named Lord Deputy of Ireland in January, 1632, where he instituted his "thorough" policy, and was arrested and imprisoned in November of 1641, just nine years and eleven months later—close enough for a poet's chronology.

In the 1648 volume, Fanshawe, by the way, has another poem entitled "On the Earl of Strafford's Trial." And a few years after Strafford's death, Fanshawe spent some two years in the home of Strafford's son (1653–55), where he translated the *Lusiads*, a translation which he dedicated to the son, saying in the epistle dedicatory, "From the hour I began [the translation] to the end thereof I slept not once out of these walls." Fanshawe was evidently a close friend of the family. I think it likely that the burial place was pointed out to him and that he actually saw the little stone of which he writes.

I am well aware of the awkward position in which a mere critic stands in correcting a great literary historian (and Sir Herbert Grierson is a great literary historian) on a point of history; but I take it that the gesture constitutes the most emphatic avowal I can make of the respect that I have for history and the most emphatic acknowledgment I can make of the extent to which the critic must rely upon history.

But having placed the poem historically, do we then possess the poem? We have considered only political history. What about the literary tradition? It is obvious that this poem is linked to a long succession of poems which moralize upon the fall from high estate. It is obvious, too, that the poem stands in a further tradition, that of the laconic epitaph, condensed, terse, and concluding with a couplet that aims at a kind of epigrammatic bite. Furthermore, as we should expect from its date, the poem makes use of some of the devices of serious wit. For example, Strafford possesses a "haplesse happy state." Here we need to have recourse to the philologists. The instance, I grant, is a humble one, requiring no more than a consultation of the dictionary, but I am mindful of the fact that the dictionary is the product of the philologist's labors. If I were teaching this poem, I should send the student to the dictionary to learn that both words come from the same root, Old Norse *hap*, meaning "good chance." The etymological linkage underscores the paradox: the very happiness (good fortune) of Strafford's state makes him a special target for his enemies and thus renders him hapless, unfortunate. We are being prepared for the later lines which describe the world's smiling on him falsely, the better to prepare him for the kill.

Thus far we have placed the poem with reference to history and to traditional themes and techniques. Are we yet in possession of the poem? We know enough about the poem now, I suppose, to pass the doctor's oral; but I think we know no more than that; and it is my general contention in this paper, of course, that the literary scholar dare not be satisfied with merely that sort of knowledge.

I have already stated that I do not think that the poem is a great poem, but I think that it is *a* poem, and if it is, it deserves more than to be fitted into its proper pigeon hole. If it is a genuine poem, it cannot be fitted into any pigeon hole.

The first lines, then, which fling "the bloudy trunck" in our faces, abruptly and shockingly point to the event. What is the commentary on the event? What is the speaker's attitude toward Strafford and toward Strafford's fate? He goes on to say, "*This little Stone* doth Seale, but not depresse." It is no grandiloquent monument, but merely a "little stone," a humiliating grave marker for a man who enjoyed royal favor. It suffices to seal the tomb but it is scarcely weighty enough to "depresse" the bloody trunk that it covers.

I am tempted to say that this third line thus echoes and reverses the paradox on "haplesse happy." The stone lies lightly upon the victim's body. It is no ponderous reminder of grandeur. One feels that the dead man can rest under it. But if it lies lightly, if it does not depress

him, it is only because it is modest and humble. Strafford
has come down from a hapless happiness to a happy
haplessness.

The poet turns the smallness of the stone, moreover,
to a further and rather startling account. The stone seems
too small to have stopped "the rowling of his fate." The
implied metaphor is that of a wheel checked in its rolling
by a stone. The wheel, surely, is fortune's wheel. Strafford
has been high on fortune's wheel, but the wheel has re-
volved with such momentum that he has been thrown
to the scaffold from his place beside the throne. Yet the
modest stone that puts a stay to his revolution is, one
feels, scarcely large enough to have checked the mighty
wheel's momentum. A great tomb, not this mere pebble
on the road of history, might suggest an obstacle large
enough to bring the rolling of so great a fate to rest.
The metaphor here may be strained, and it is possible that
I am making far too much of the little stone, though I
I am conscious only of trying to indicate what the poet
makes of it. At any rate, the stone that Fanshawe had
in mind was actually small, for Lady Burghclere, writing
in 1931, was unable to find it. She states that Strafford's
body was borne home "so quietly for fear that the . . .
brutish multitude might vent their spite on his corpse,
that the place of his burying remains a mystery."

In my revulsion from the passivity that Yeats condemns,
I may have displayed too much activity, even a fantastic
agility. I hope that this audience will not feel that in
going out to meet the poem, I have gone much more than
the stipulated halfway and have actually lugged the poem
home on my own shoulders, reading my own meaning
into the poem rather than Fanshawe's out of it. Yet

this first stanza is packed with meaning. We are bound
to try to encompass it; and at any event the ironic meaning of the all-too-modest gravestone does become the
matter of the second stanza.

If justice has denied to Strafford a tomb of brass,
common pity for his virtues builds in our minds a tomb
more nearly worthy of him, an imaginary vault. This
imaginary tomb is actually stronger than brass, and time
will strive in vain to raze it. Such imaginary tombs had
been built earlier by William Browne for the Countess of
Pembroke, and by John Milton for Shakespeare's bones.
But if we wish to trace sources and parallels, we can go
far back of Fanshawe's contemporaries. If someone, for example, wants to suggest that Fanshawe is thinking of
Horace's *Exegi Monumentum Aere Perrenius*, I shall have
to agree with him at once. As a matter of fact, Fanshawe
actually translated that ode of Horace. His translation
begins:

> A Work out-lasting Brass and higher
> Then Regal Pyramid's proud Spire,
> I have absolv'd. Which storming Winds,
> The Sea that Turrets undermines,
> Tract of innumerable daies,
> Nor the rout of Time can raze.

This last line echoes, as you will have noticed, the eighth
line of our poem, ". . . time strives in vaine to raze."

But the conjecture that Fanshawe here is probably
remembering Horace, interesting though it may be, does
not settle for us the success or lack of success of this
second stanza. He may have given us in this second stanza
a vain and empty conceit. For my own part, I think that

the stanza is excellent. In the context established, the metaphor is not hyperbolical but ironic and conveys a sense of accurate and even restrained statement. The tomb we raise is an insubstantial shadow of the brazen vault, an imaginary vault, yet because imaginary, the only tomb capable of withstanding the assault of time.

It should be apparent that these first eight lines are very important for the whole poem. They suggest the attitude to be taken toward Strafford, whose happy state was actually hapless, whose burial stone, in view of the career which it closes, is niggardly; and they comment upon the quality of justice which denied him a better memorial. But the speaker has developed the attitude in terms of his imagery, quietly and almost without overt comment. These first eight lines coil the spring, as it were, store up the driving power of the poem for its ultimate release. The third stanza can thus proceed rapidly through a summary of the actual events: "Ten yeares the world upon him falsly smild," etc. And the concluding couplet, releasing the spring, can come home with sudden power:

> Then threw him to a Scaffold from a Throne.
> *Much Doctrine lyes under this little Stone.*

By this time, the phrase "little stone" has been charged: it has the whole of the poem back of it. The much doctrine that it conveys is not some elaborate epitaph inscribed *upon* it. The fact that circumstances do not allow anything to be carved upon the stone is itself eloquent. The doctrine lies *under* the stone, and that doctrine becomes the more impressive because it does not need to be stated, because the reader, prepared as he has been by the ex-

perience of the whole poem, can formulate the doctrine
for himself.

I am not at all sure that I have succeeded in making the
poem come alive for you, or in describing the kind of
life that the poem possesses. The poem may remain for
you merely one of the gorier beheaded figures in period
costume in Madame Tussaud's Wax Works. But I hope
that I have suggested the goal to be achieved, even if
I have failed to demonstrate the achievement.

For though Strafford's bones moulder now under his
little stone, and though Sir Richard Fanshawe has gone
to join him years ago, Fanshawe's *poem* is not a corpse.
It is still very much alive. Of that I am certain. The study
of literature must deal with that life.

I have not, however, quite done with my illustration
yet. I must tell you that this poem, which was certainly
not written on the death of Charles I, and which I have
argued—persuasively, I hope—alludes to the death of
Strafford, is, in fact, a translation of a Spanish sonnet
by Luis de Góngora. Góngora's sonnet commemorates
the death of his friend, Rodrigo Calderon, who was long
a favorite at the Spanish court but eventually fell from
power and was beheaded in 1621, some twenty years
before Strafford's fall. Fanshawe resided in Spain for a
number of years during the 1630's, became acquainted
with Góngora's work, and published translations of a
number of his poems.

What happens, then, to the pretty case we have built
up for Strafford? Where does this leave us? Well, actually
it leaves us very close to where we were. Fanshawe's
translation is close, but not slavish, and he makes some
significant changes in Góngora's poem. The emphasis on

the meager stone is almost wholly Fanshawe's contribution. More significantly, Fanshawe has altered Góngora's "quatro lustros," four lustrums, that is to say, twenty years, to "Ten yeares the world upon him falsly smild." I suspect that when Fanshawe came to write his poem on Strafford, he remembered Góngora's sonnet and decided to make it the basis of his poem; or, alternatively, that having translated Góngora's poem, he so altered it as to make it apply to Strafford's case. In view of all the evidence, I am willing to let stand my earlier contention for a definite reference to Strafford.

But let us suppose that Góngora's friend had enjoyed, like Strafford, just ten years of favor, not twenty. Suppose further that the two cases were so exactly similar that there was no way to determine whether Fanshawe was thinking of Strafford or merely translating Góngora. What then? The case for Strafford would have to go, I think. The most that we could say would be that Fanshawe might possibly have been thinking of Strafford as he translated. But an exceedingly hypothetical thought in the poet's mind is a very frail peg on which to hang a poem. True. But the poem does not hang from such a peg. Withdrawing the historical and personal references does not destroy the poem. If the poem was a good poem when attached to Strafford, it is still a good poem when detached from him. The poem is not altered in the least. For the poem is not a passive mirror into which we peek to discover the features of the Earl of Strafford or the face of a Spanish grandee or even the bloody head of King Charles. I hope that I have already given testimony to my interest in the poem as a historical document. But the critic's concern is finally with the poem as a poem.

The critic's concern is not inimical to the historian's, but it goes beyond it, and properly so. In teaching the poem, the references to Strafford do serve as a device for getting one's students into the poem. But I think that, facing a class of sophomores, I could make do with an analogy from the newspapers, making Mr. Forrestal, say, play Strafford to President Truman's King Charles.[1]

These last remarks, however, may suggest that in my fear lest the poem become a mere corpse of all-too-solid flesh, I am substituting for it a boneless wraith, an insubstantial ghost. That is, my last remarks could be misinterpreted as a glorification of impressionism and subjective judgment. The scholars of the last generation distrusted, quite properly, I think, mere emoting over the work of art. The more extrinsic scholarly disciplines are sometimes justified as being valuable because they are extrinsic and objective, not subjectively irresponsible and vague. It is in just this connection that the passage that I quoted earlier from Yeats can be extremely useful. For Yeats's own poetry, in rejecting passivity before a mechanized nature, does not go off into emotional irresponsibility. Far from it. Yeats's great poems are emotionally responsible; and if they resist treatment as logical documents, it is not because they violate logic, but because they transcend it. They are in fact rigorously disciplined. "Sailing to Byzantium" or "Among School Children" are not reveries or irresponsible day dreams. It behooves the teacher of literature to comprehend, and to enable others to comprehend, the discipline which gives them order. This is what his role as literary scholar and critic specific-

___

[1] This paper was given some months before James Forrestal's tragic death.

ally enjoins him to do. His task is to put the student in possession of the poem.

To sum up: if this obligation is not to be discharged by the scholar's merely collecting the facts *about* the poem, neither is it discharged by his testifying to how powerfully the poem affected him. His own prose poem about the beauty of the poem will probably be poor poetry; it certainly will not be criticism. To discharge his obligation he needs to induct his student into the poem as an imaginative structure. It is not an easy task. One often learns with dismay how badly he has misread a poem or a novel; or realizes that in attempting to say what a given poem "says," he has given only his own warped reading of it. But to evade the problem in favor of some "objective" comment is simply to dodge the problem because it is difficult.

We come back at this point to Yeats's analysis of the situation, the analysis with which we began. The concept which presents us with verifiable objectivity on the one hand and private, and therefore irresponsible, subjectivity on the other is the very falsification about which Yeats was writing. The question is begged at the start. We begin with a concept of literature which, by denying the creative imagination, denies the structural principle of works of the imagination. We start with a false dilemma. We get, on the one hand, mechanized nature, amenable to scientific description, and we get on the other, the realm of judgment and value, private and unverifiable. It is the split that runs through our Western civilization. It is indeed the breach which the scientists themselves, now alarmed at the state of our culture, are appealing to the humanities to heal. But the crack goes right down through the humanities themselves. It is the fissure which splits many an English department wide open. Intellect is split off from emotion; facts from values; scholarship from criticism; research from teaching. There are the facts about the document to be checked and tested. Objective verification is possible. There is, on the other hand, emotion, vague and nebulous. And so we have the solid research scholar and the inspirational, evangelical lecturer; or we have the instructor who is "brilliant but"—that is, brilliant, and as a necessary consequence, unsound. Or we have the frustrated poet who works away at his footnotes through the day, but having slammed the drawer shut on his tools, later in the evening weeps into his beer over the sad death of Percy Shelley.

It is high time to reject a conception of literature which forces this dichotomy upon us. We need to realize our proper function. We need to stop aping the physical scientists, who long ago became bored with the compliment. The best of them are urging us to be ourselves. We need to remind ourselves that we profess to teach an art.

If this seems a lame conclusion, I remind you that it will seem lame only in so far as we are still under the spell of the concept that I am urging us to throw off—a concept which vests truth in science and sees in literature only a kind of effeminate prettification. In manly revulsion from this conception, some scholars and critics have attempted to import values from ethics, or economics, or politics. The muse is to become a rewrite girl—in the 'twenties for the values of the new humanists, in the 'thirties for the Marxists, in the 'forties for a program of liberal-democratic values. I sympathize with such scholars. Our civilization is in a bad way. I share their sense of the urgency to *do* something about it. But I reflect that we can do *our most* about it by doing well our specific job: by keeping open the lines of communication with the realm of value; by re-establishing, in a language which is fast breaking down into abstract formula or else into gobbledygook, the capacity to communicate values; by exercising to health the now half-atrophied faculties by which man apprehends value. This is not the least important of tasks. It will seem unimportant only to the man who has made a superficial diagnosis of the sickness of our culture. A more profound diagnosis will see this as one of the essential tasks. Somebody had better undertake it. I submit that it is the task for which we who teach the humanities are peculiarly responsible.

2 The Humanities and the Common Reader

Howard Mumford Jones

THE HUMANITIES, whatever is meant by that baffling term, seem to the musing observer to offer a succession of paradoxes. The word itself is a modern invention, coming to us from the nineteenth century. One might reasonably infer that, given so recent a coinage, we must know what we mean by it. In fact, however, we do not quite know what we mean by it, and this is the first paradox. We believe in something we cannot delimit. Probably the only safe working definition of the humanities is this: "You know horses—cows are different." You know the sciences, the humanities are different. They are what you have left in the college curriculum when you extract the sciences—natural, physical, and social.

Or are they? Huxley was neither the first nor the last great man to claim that science, nobly pursued, offers a humane mode of education, and I, for one, am quite ready to admit his claim. As for the social sciences, if the object of humane learning is man; and if man is, as he seemed to Aristotle to be, a political animal; and if the social sciences have anything wise to say about him as a political animal, and I think they do, I find it difficult to keep up the proper humanistic irreverence for the social sciences. For example, I am not convinced that sociology is any more plagued by jargon than is philological lore, literary criticism, or contemporary aesthetics. Novelists and poets there have been who were also wise men, but novelists and poets are not always wise, and I am unable to grasp the logic which argues that because Plato and Shakespeare are wise men, therefore contemporary social psychologists must be shallow and wrong. This is too much like scorning the typewriter because it was not used by Homer.

Is history one of the humanities, or is it one of the social sciences? Is the theory of the state in Dante to be considered forever valuable because it is in literary form, whereas cultural anthropology is to remain only a passing fashionable craze? Sometimes humanistic scholars argue as if they thought so. May I remind you of a scholar named Francis Bacon who, seeing great hopes for mankind in empirical science, also said that undue reverence for "authority" is one of the peccant humors of learning?

We do not, then, really know what we mean by the humanities, and this very uncertainty perhaps leads us to be a little bit arrogant about our claims for our own priority in wisdom. We do not, in fact, really know whether we can distinguish a peculiar body of lore or wisdom or organized knowledge as something uniquely ours. Of course the professional humanist will seldom admit that this is so, but in fact I think it *is* so, and I am inclined to believe that a little more intellectual humility among scholars in discussing each other's specialties would be a valuable practical example of the ripe fruits of humane discipline.

But let me pass to a second paradox. If it is hard to separate humane learning from all other sorts of learning, another contradiction puzzles me. The humanities, whatever else they are, are highly educational, so much so that they have their principal, and perhaps their only,

home in educational institutions, whereas the sciences
spill over into industry and government, and the social
sciences spill over into business, government, and social
welfare. If the colleges and universities were to shut down
tomorrow, I think the sciences and the social sciences,
though they would be injured, could get along, but in
that event I am not clear that the humanities could get
along, unless they took refuge in public libraries. They
are, it would seem, quintessentially bookish and also quintessentially part of the educational process. The great humanists, the great humanist documents prove ever and
again to be consciously educational.

This being so, a man from Mars might reasonably infer that education, particularly education in the democratic state, a state wherein the responsibilities for decision
rest, even if they rest indirectly, upon every citizen, would
be a matter of primary concern to humanists. He would
infer, for example, that if there is a subject called education, if the training of teachers seems essential to the
health of the commonwealth, education must be one of
the humanities, and the enlisting, training, and honoring
of teachers, particularly public school teachers, would be
of immediate concern to humanists. I need not remind
you, however, that the man from Mars is in for a terrible
shock. He will discover that professional educational training is carried forward in special schools for which all good
humanists express unmitigated contempt, that when
school teachers come into humanistic courses for training,
as they do in our summer sessions, it is fashionable to
treat them with a sort of good-humored tolerance, and
that you do not awaken any genuine pedagogical enthusiasm in the humanist unless you propose that he train

young persons to be scholars like himself. Then, indeed, his zeal awakes, then he really dedicates himself to an educational cause, the cause of the graduate school. Yet so remote in fact is the responsibility, even then, for any direct educational training among humanistic research workers that the graduate schools of the country have, until very recently, refused to recognize that young doctors of philosophy in the humanities are not going directly into research libraries, but into classrooms where their first job is to teach high school graduates, the majority of whom are not going to be humanistic specialists.

The scholar, of course, has his defense. The defense is that those pernicious and windy fellows, the professors of education, do not understand subject matter, but only formulae. They teach teachers to teach. This the humanist will not do. For him, teaching is a by-product. Teaching is something you learn to do indirectly, through some professional trade secret not revealed to any but the catechumens. And with this excoriation of schools of education and of the badness of our civil pedagogy, the humanist rests his case.

I venture to suggest that the greatest teachers of mankind—Buddha, Socrates, Jesus, Epictetus, Tolstoy, Emerson, whom you will—got along rather well without a Ph.D. They had no printed bibliographies, they demanded no term papers, and they were not, like Charles Eliot Norton, overwhelmed by melancholy because there were no gentlemen in the class. They seem to have concerned themselves, so far as I can make out, rather directly with the education of what we quaintly call the common man and with the training of teachers to teach him. They commanded their followers to become fishers of men rather than fishers of symbolic logic, or aesthetics, or philology, or the *Cambridge Bibliography of English Literature*. And if I am shamelessly, in this question-begging manner, taking advantage of your good nature by a preposterous collocation of unlike things, it is not because I do not respect the *Cambridge Bibliography of English Literature*, philological learning, greatness in art, and the ontological argument for God. Rather, what I am trying to do is to shock you into a sense of how the aristocratic spirit which lurks in scholarship, the samurai spirit of specialism, has carried us away from the rather central problem of the education of the human race.

And this skillfully brings me to my third paradox. To make it clear, I am going to talk for a time as if literary studies and the humanities were interchangeable terms, which they are not, and I am going to seem to find fault with a book which, in fact, I admire. This book is *Theory of Literature* by Messrs. Wellek and Warren, published last winter, a clear, careful, compact, perspicuous cyclopaedia from which you can learn where we stand today in the theory and practice of the higher study of one of the arts. The authors seem to have read and digested everything. There is, for instance, a chapter on the study of euphony, rhythm, and meter, and it is a good chapter. There is one on style and stylistics—I had to find out that this last term is a technical word for investigations into "all devices which aim at some specific expressive end and thus [it] embraces far more than literature or even rhetoric." In this chapter you will find succinct accounts of where we stand today in our knowledge of matters like "expressive value," "sentence pattern," the analysis of linguistic systems, sound schemes, periphrastic vocabularies, and like technical problems. In a world which includes, as Robinson says, both bugs and emperors, there is room for this sort of study, and I am glad it is intelligently pursued. There are other chapters on literary history; on the ordering and establishing of evidence; on image, metaphor, symbol, and myth; on literary genres; and on the study of literature at the graduate level. This ends with an admirable, if familiar, plea:

> We need not longer maintain [the] nineteenth-century epistemology or accept the dismissal of the arts as no longer deserving of serious attention. . . . We professors of literature must not hope to persist in our old, easy ways, our personal compoundings of pedantry and dilettantism. Literary study within our universities—our teaching and writing—must become purposively literary. It must turn away from the delightful details of "research" and direct itself to the large, unsolved problems of literary history and literary theory. It must receive stimulation and direction from modern criticism and contemporary literature—from participation in literature as a living institution.

Obviously, this is well said. I have, it may be, my private doubts whether we shall ever solve the large unsolved problems of literary history and literary theory (if we did, I don't know what would become of the Modern Language Association), and I must protest that I have not, myself, found my professional way of life particularly easy, nor have I discovered many colleagues justly chargeable with either dilettantism or pedantry.

Pedantry, indeed, can be defined only as it refers to somebody else's scholarship. But by and large we can accept the exordium—up to its last phrase: "literature as a living institution." What *is* literature as a living institution? Or, to bring the matter home, what *is* literature as a living institution in the United States?

Perhaps the book will tell us. I open it at the chapter entitled "Image, Metaphor, Symbol, Myth" and read at random this passage:

> Rhetoricians like Quintilian already make much of the distinction between the metaphor which animates the inanimate, and that which inanimates the animate; but they present the distinction as one between rhetorical devices. With [Dr. Hermann] Pongs . . . it becomes a grandiose contrast between polar attitudes—that of the mythic imagination, which projects personality upon the outer world of things, which animizes and animates nature, and the contrary type of imagination, which feels its way into the alien, which de-animizes or unsubjectivizes itself. All the possibilities of figurative expression are exhausted by these two, the subjective and objective poles.

A footnote tells us that Dr. Pongs "calls the first of his types the *Beseeltypus* and the second the *Erfühltypus*. The first animizes or anthropomorphizes; the second emphasizes."

Is this literature, is this literary study as a living institution in the United States? The answer is not easy, but it is not necessarily "no," nor am I trying to ridicule

Dr. Pongs, or Quintilian, or Messrs. Wellek and Warren. Within its own universe of discourse, this somewhat complex prose makes perfectly good sense; and as there should somewhere be a group of persons, however small, passionately devoted to metaphor and style, I should, for one, vigorously defend Dr. Pongs's right to a theory, just as I should vigorously defend Messrs. Wellek and Warren for presenting this theory in clear and admirable English. But if it be true that to a tiny fraction of our population the problem of whether metaphor animizes or de-animizes discourse is a matter of absorbing interest, it is also patent that to the vaster proportion of our population, this problem is of no interest whatsoever. And this vast majority, though it includes the ignorant and the illiterate and the barbarian, includes also the majority of educated men and women, to whom books and the pleasure of reading are part of an intelligent and cultivated life. The patrons of our bookstores, the readers of our weekly book reviews, the members of the various book-of-the-month clubs, the subscribers to rental libraries, and, in sum, the whole body of our reading public, without whose sanction there can be no literature at all, have, with obvious but rare exceptions, no interest in this talk about polar attitudes, mythic imagination, and unsubjectivizing metaphors. They are willing to have this sort of thing in the schools out of a blind and flattering belief that scholarship is beyond them anyway and that this bookish theoric is all well enough for the university classroom and for something mysterious called "learning."

Well, that there should be something mysterious called learning is something no wise man will dispute. But learning for what? Learning for whom? Learning to what rele-

vant end? The vocabulary of Messrs. Wellek and Warren
is admirable for purposes of learning, in the sense that it
is intelligible to learned men. But it is also a technological
vocabulary, the product of some decades of scholarly research, which is in its way as incomprehensible to the
cultivated reader as is the vocabulary of nuclear physics.
In fact, we have as scholars been carrying on a series of
technical operations in language and literature so delicate
and complex that it takes the neophyte a long time merely
to master the significance of the words we use. And lat-
terly, especially in the twentieth century, we have carried
our technical operations out of what we vaguely call scholarship into what we vaguely call criticism. Thus, from a
recent anthology of criticism I cull such phrases as these:
"the sporadic intuition of artists," "controlling feeling
through metaphor," "the ideal spectator," "details that
are lyrically impure," "pseudo-reference," "the poem is
oblique," "a certain degree of contradiction between tenor
and vehicle," "scraps fuse into integer," "rich and in-
tuitive use of Christian imagery," unable "to say what
machinery erects a staircase on a contradiction," "ironic
tension in poetry," "simultaneity of perception . . . by
breaking up temporal sequence." These are characteristic
phrases, picked at random. Of course I do them injustice;
of course, by taking them out of context, I have given
them a nudity they do not deserve; of course, if the critic
is to penetrate far into the subtle psychology of the creative process and the perceptive mind, the old, worn critical
phrases will not do, and he must invent new ones. But it
is precisely to the quality of these invented phrases that
I call your attention. To the common reader, most of
these phrases—excellent no doubt in their places in the

essays which contain them, casting for the adept few a real light on literary subtleties—most of these phrases are as opaque as the vocabulary of higher mathematics. And he concludes that if the literary experts are thus unable to make things clear to him, why should he bother with them? However intense and serious to the academician the theory of criticism may seem to be, to the many, books are still a recreation, are for one's idle times, are, indeed, a luxury. What they want out of books is delight and guidance, not conundrums.

I am far from saying that the common reader is necessarily right. If anybody wants to murmur that there is no royal road to humanistic learning, I shall not object. Nevertheless, literary scholarship and literary criticism have grown into curiously technological affairs; and from what little I know about aesthetic theory now governing painting and music, this is also becoming technological, at least from the point of view of the common listener, the common beholder. And, as I once occupied a penthouse owned by an expert in symbolic logic, I can testify, from having tried to read in his library, that large areas of modern metaphysical speculation seem to be more technological still. The one branch of the humanities which has not developed this technological density seems to be history. I find it possible to read history, just as the common reader reads it, with my expectation of plain communication between writer and reader amply fulfilled.

Confronting this implied reproach, the humanist may retort that he has no monopoly on technological talk. If this be an offense, he may say, scientists offend more deeply. But here, I think, we must distinguish. The technological talk of the scientists is aimed at other scientists;

it does not pretend, like literary criticism or books on ethics or treatises on art, to be aimed also at the general reader. The universe of discourse of the natural and physical sciences grows daily more complex and requires a complex vocabulary in which to communicate its ideas, whereas there is no special reason to suppose that the psychology of artistic creation has changed a very great deal since the time of the Greeks or to believe that the general principles of morality and metaphysics have in a thousand years undergone very much of a revolution. Men are still nominalists or realists, monists or dualists, believers in empiricism or trusters in the absolute, theists, atheists, materialists, skeptics, or agnostics as they were in Athens or Alexandria. For if the thoughts of the mighty dead are, indeed, obsolete, we have been wasting a great many valuable man-hours in the classroom pretending that antiquarianism was life itself. The humanist cannot have it both ways. He cannot insist that the works of the past are still virtually as valuable as ever they were and simultaneously declare that these works have never been understood until, equipped with modern criticism, modern philology, modern scholarship, truth dawns on us here in the United States in the year nineteen hundred and what you please. I do not deny that some among us know a great deal more about the middle ages than did the eighteenth century dilettanti or that our views of the classical past are in all probability juster than those which prevailed at the court of Charles the Great. But are the insights, the values, the canons of the common reader any juster? This, from the point of view of the health of a liberal society, is truly the question to put to the humanists. And if the scholar says that what he does at the top of the intellectual pyramid will, he hopes, trickle down to the masses at the bottom, the common reader cannot but think that trickling down is a rather amateurish, not to say uncertain, mode of distributing the treasures the humanists claim to have stored up for him.

The common reader has, indeed, been standing patiently by while I have gone off on this long excursion suggested by the admirable volume of Messrs. Wellek and Warren. Who is the common reader? He (or she) is the common voter, the high school graduate, the college alumnus, the sober citizen who gives what he can to the Community Fund, tries to weigh the claims of contending parties for his vote, participates in meetings of the Parent-Teachers' Association, supports the colleges (and incidentally the humanists) through his gifts and taxes, and tries, by subscribing to magazines and reading books, to inform himself about men, manners, and opinions. For him, incorrigibly if you like, a novel is supposed to tell a story. For him, regrettably perhaps, poetry is expected to support or to console; and if he can make nothing out of sprung rhythm or Mr. Eliot's "Four Quartets," he has read, let us say, *A Shropshire Lad* and he likes—as who does not? —Benet's fine narrative poem, *John Brown's Body*. As for philosophy, I am afraid he is, or at any rate his wife is, a reader of Rabbi Liebman's *Peace of Mind*, which he has bought in great quantities, just as he has bought Mr. Churchill's memoirs and Mr. Sherwood's book on Harry Hopkins. If a Shakespeare play comes along, let us say Olivier's film of *Hamlet*, he is likely to go to it with his wife and to have some rather fresh views on the production; and I have even seen him in the gallery of a modern art show and sat next to him at a symphony concert. By and large, in the long run, directly or indirectly, he is, is he not, the man whom, in the liberal state, our humanistic studies are primarily designed to influence. We can of course pretend that humanistic scholarship is supported now as it has been supported in the past by wealthy aristocrats, but by and large this is no longer true, and the support of patrons as questionable as Catherine the Great, Pope Alexander VI, or Alcibiades, to stick to the safely dead, is, I have always thought, a rather awkward argument for humanism. No, our present wealth is the wealth of foundations giving out money for social ends, our institutions are tax-supported or kept alive by social campaigns among the alumni, and we are, in sum, committed for our lives and fortunes to the belief of the common reader that we somehow do him good.

I agree that we do him good. We keep alive something called a tradition. We have a great amount of "knowledge about," which is sometimes almost a substitute for knowledge. We help to civilize his offspring, and we persuade a tiny fraction of them to become scholars like ourselves. Without us, the common reader's knowledge of the past would be nebulous indeed. But I am not persuaded, and I think the common reader is not persuaded, that we have richly fulfilled the duties tradition lays upon us.

I do not quite know what is meant by that vague word "tradition." But I suggest, in the light of the considerations I have urged, that it is not so much the humanist tradition which should concern us as it is the traditional humanist. He has, like the god Janus, a double face. He is simultaneously teacher and scholar. Each of his functions is necessary, the one having its obligation primarily to the learning without which modern society cannot exist, the other having its obligation primarily to society, without which learning cannot exist. But I suggest that the development of our expertized culture has developed the first of these functions out of all proportion to our needs and that we need now to return upon the other function and see what we can do to enrich it for ordinary people —for, to continue my metaphor, the common reader.

The paradox of learning, or rather of the learned man, is patently that in proportion as his expert knowledge increases, his general range diminishes, or is likely to diminish unless he is a very great man indeed. So-and-so has his specialty—American literature, baroque art, literary criticism, Hegelian metaphysics, Alexandrian inscriptions from India—and he naturally desires to enrich his knowledge and to convey his enthusiasm to others. Hence the extraordinary rise of specialisms in American universities, which, if they have increased "knowledge about," have not necessarily increased knowledge, because too often they diminish judgment. They diminish judgment by virtue of the fact that book, document, or object is perpetually interposed as a screen between judgment and direct experience of life. In truth, to change the figure, as our lore grows in quantity, we resemble an army with a baggage train constantly increasing, so that we drag at each remove a lengthening chain.

Efforts to correct this evil—and evil it is—efforts to plunge the masterpiece once more into the living stream of experience from whence it once took form, are constant and commendable. They appear as heroic simplifications —great books, general education, "criticism," the history of culture, the tutorial system, an honors seminar—and it would be idle to deny that these changes have accom-

plishment to their credit. But they are nevertheless altera-
tions in pattern and machinery; they do not drive directly
enough at men. They do not, in sum, guarantee us the
kind of teacher we need.

The teacher: whence comes he? How find him? How
train him? How persuade him steadfastly to believe that
the living personality has an enchantment the library,
with all its magic, can never own? Dr. Johnson reminded
his readers that if Shakespeare's practice was contrary to
the rules of criticism, there was always an appeal open
from criticism to nature; and it is in the inability to make
the appeal from theory to nature that humanistic teaching is principally at fault. We are bound up with our own
books. We do not sufficiently inquire whether the poem,
the string quartet, the sculpture, the canvas is likely to
please many and please long by its just representation of
general nature in terms which the intelligent, but not expert, beholder can be pleased with; we are so deeply absorbed by category and technique, form and pattern that
we cannot put down the book except to run to another
book in order to bulwark our judgment. Our weakness is
to mistake debate among scholars for that appeal to general nature which Johnson made the test of Shakespeare's
greatness. And note that Johnson tested the quality of
greatness by general nature and not, as too many specialists do, general nature by the quality of bookish greatness.

All parts of the university feel the want of teachers, but
this defect is most signal among the humanities. To discuss whether present patterns in education among our
graduate schools are likely to produce teachers and to re-
vivify the notion of the teacher as a man speaking to man
would take us far afield. Not philology, not criticism, not

accuracy, not bibliographical range, not casuistry, not expert knowledge of iconography or of musical form, each excellent in itself, offers inherent guarantee that a new and powerful teacher has stepped upon the stage of the world. Nor, at the other extreme, is a sentimental aversion to intellectual thoroughness any better guarantee. The teacher is not book-bound, but a lover of life. He is unmoved by the psychology of terror or dispute. He reads every scripture in the light of the times which brought it forth, but he does not therefore mistake past prejudice and present fashion for eternity. His faith is life, not the shadow of life cast by the arts, glorious though they are in certain moods and hours. He does not dwell on the seacoast of Bohemia. He knows that books are good, that pictures, music, systems, language are good also, but that they are for times and seasons. If the exquisite and the exotic appeal, if intellectual dexterity has its glitter and its charm, he remains unshaken in the observation that the great human issues are common, coarse and solid; as, death, birth, sex, children, food. He breathes not in the thin air of libraries, decanting out-of-print comedy, tragedy, realism, and romance; instead, if he be dark of soul, his pessimism is bracing, and if of another stripe of spirit, he gives out a joyful and enduring sagacity. Gladly he accepts the injunction of Turgenief: "Simplify! simplify!" since, without derogating from the specialists, he is also enough of a child of Lincoln to know that, in one sense at least, it is in the general classroom that we shall greatly win or meanly lose the last best hope of man.

This is, I know, that rhetoric which blurs distinctions; yet if the humanist tradition springs from the spirit of man, how shall we discourse of the great teacher except spiritually? But that you may not dismiss me as a mere poet, I offer two concrete suggestions for the improvement of the tradition of humanistic teaching. The first is that we radically reduce the number of persons to be admitted to our graduate schools for professional humanistic training, and by this reduction achieve, I hope, a competition for place which will gradually weed out those blameless mediocrities now furnishing too large a fraction of our Ph.D.'s. If we really went at the problem of admitting students to graduate training as the Guggenheim Foundation goes at the problem of ascertaining what ten among a hundred applicants are worth the human energy about to be expended on them; if by interview and test, evidence of others, and performance by the candidate we undertook to screen our catechumens with half the intelligence that publishers use to award prizes or that juries employ in awarding certain famous fellowships, we should not wonder long that humanistic teaching is flaccid and jejune. Our mistaken kindness is twofold: the fact that anybody wants to study under us is flattering; the moral excellence of the applicant (usually conceived of negatively), is wrongly regarded as a surrogate for moral vigor, intellectual achievement, and emotional stability.

My second practical suggestion is equally simple, equally revolutionary, and equally logical. If humanistic studies deal with the whole man, let us ascertain that we have the whole man before us to educate. The soundest part of the theory of Cecil Rhodes, whatever its deficiencies in administration, was that which insisted on the wholeness of personality among the applicants. The test in that case was sometimes prowess in sports, sometimes school leadership, sometimes another trait or quality, but the test was right in intent. It seems to me of less moment with respect to a particular graduate student whether his grades in book courses are A's and B's than that he should be a healthy human animal with a sense of humor, skill at the piano, the ability to play baseball, a capacity to take long walks, and the training that will enable him to know good food from bad and cheap whisky from civilized drinking. But if you do not like these particular traits and regard them as whimsical, I beg you to set up such of your own as will guarantee in reasonable measure that you are not creating another unhappy bookworm. For, in truth, I know no way to avoid the excess of specialism except to avoid it, and the best way to begin avoiding it is to assure yourself that the human material you are about to deal with is sound, not morbid; humorous and forthright, not withdrawn; somebody, in short, somewhere near capable of fulfilling all the offices both public and private, whether of peace or of war.

3 The Critic and his Text
A Clarification and a Defense

Cleanth Brooks

Some of you will recall that in my first paper I tried to point out some of the relationships of criticism to literary scholarship, stressing the extent to which criticism leans heavily upon scholarship, but arguing that *literary* scholarship is barren unless it is informed by criticism. Nearly everything that I said in delivering that paper has been very ably and systematically said at considerable length in that remarkable book recently published, *Theory of Literature* by René Wellek and Austin Warren. I think that much that I propose to say in the next few minutes is also to be found explicitly or by implication in that same book. I recommend it to this group. For much that I shall not have time to say in a brief paper is said there, with the extensions of the argument, the reservations, the qualifications, and the elaborations of a position that can be set forth here only very briefly.

In my previous paper I was primarily concerned with the relation of criticism to scholarship. At present I am concerned with the relation of formal criticism to the study of the psychology of composition and to the study of the sociological and political effects of literature. In this instance, the attack on formal criticism comes not so much from the vested academic interests as from the avant-garde literary people and from the vested interests of the literary journalists. The critic is damned not for what he does but rather for his apparent lack of concern for certain burning problems.

I can paraphrase the typical comment in this way. The critic is off in his corner doing his close textual analysis and forgetting the urgent and chaotic world about him. He is fiddling—fiddling around with paltry words—while Manhattan is burning down. The avant-garde writer wants the critic to tell him how to write a poem or how to write a novel—not *him*, of course, for quite properly the avant-garde writer would not take his advice anyway. Nevertheless, the problem of writing the poem or novel is the urgent problem for him and it irritates him exceedingly that the critic is very obviously being of no help at all.

Mr. J. Donald Adams, on the other hand, is perpetually angry because the formal critic, absorbed in his own pettifogging concern with words, is not giving the country proper morals; or if we take a cut higher in the scale, the so-called crisis critics belabor him for not giving more attention to America's pervasive obsession with guilt, or the *Partisan Review* spanks him for neglecting the Existentialist situation—or has the line now changed?—at any rate, for neglecting whatever the *Partisan Review* current concern happens to be.

I think that all these attacks share certain common misconceptions. But none of them, I dare say, is held by all the individuals who attack formal criticism, and the misconceptions are stressed in varying degrees. Since, in order to save time, I must lump all these related attacks together, I call your attention to the fact that what I shall say is not meant to apply necessarily to any one individual or group.

1. The charges have in common an unconscious contempt for words. We are all good Americans in assuming that words themselves are thin husks for ideas and sensations, and we easily get out of patience at the very idea that someone is wasting time over them. I grant that some of us do merely waste time in attempting to deal with them; however, the irate attack on the "new critics" hardly distinguishes between fruitful concern with the text and a pedantic and empty concern.

2. These attacks have in common a sense of urgency in the realization that all is not well with our culture. The realization has to be put down to the credit of the observers, but the deterioration that is going on is hardly going to be stopped by the critics, even if they should turn moralists and social engineers.

3. The attacks also have in common the misconception that literature can substitute for religion, a hope that goes back at least to Matthew Arnold. If literature can give us the values that religion once gave, then, so the unconscious reasoning goes, the critic ought to be a kind of literary theologian, or at least a popular preacher. I think that literature is tremendously important, but I do not think that it can substitute for religion. I think that one is likely to get a shabby literature and a shabby religion if the two are confused. And therefore, though I am sorry for the boys who hold a protest meeting on the naked shingle of Dover Beach, I am forced to conclude that their imprecations merely reverse King Canute's. I do not think that literature will give them the high tide for which they beg, though I think it may give them propaganda novels and social documents. Serious literature can merely show them their own plight.

4. Since those who attack criticism hold a confused view of what literature is, they commit the intentional fallacy or the affective fallacy, or usually both. I use the terms developed by Beardsley and Wimsatt in their two brilliant recent articles. The intentional fallacy makes the meaning of the poem determined by the author's intention; the affective fallacy judges the goodness of the poem by the audience's response. Thus a novel by Thomas Wolfe must be good because Thomas Wolfe was a buoyant and powerful personality and was intending to express America in the novel discussed. Now, the novel discussed may in fact be very good; but we have no right, in literature, to take the thought for the deed, and we get some very curious results if we try to do so. The literary morgue is paved with good intentions even as are the floors of hell.

The affective fallacy holds that the poem or novel is good because it made Mr. Housman's skin so bristle that the razor, though bidden, would not perform its office. Or it holds that the novel or poem is good because forty million Americans cannot be wrong in their fervent reactions to it.

Now I do not mean to be pedantic, to force everyone to speak by the card. All of us from time to time drop into the intentional or the affective fallacies—as we express our likes and dislikes, and as we comment upon the values of various literary works. But serious discussions of literature are invalid in so far as they make use of these fallacies. I think that Messrs. Wimsatt and Beardsley prove their case up to the hilt. That case amounts to this: logically the intentional fallacy takes us away from the work of literature to the study of the author's letters and diaries, or more logically still, if we can get it, to the author's sworn statement under oath as to what he intended to say. The affective fallacy also logically takes us away from consideration of the literary document to the offices of the Gallup poll, or to the manipulator of the lie-detector machine, where we can get measurable, objective data on the person's blood pressure and heart-beat rate as he reads the work in question.

Yet, since these fallacies are widespread, a critic who undertakes to examine the text of a poem or novel with care does seem, naturally, to be indulging in a piddling activity. Small wonder that he has been damned for possessing an Alexandrian preoccupation with minutiae.

5. In general, however, the attack on formal criticism holds as its dearest assumption this: the assumption that all of us can read a work of art and read it accurately. I wish that we could. But it is my considered opinion that most of us do it inadequately and, conditioned as we are by our particular civilization, it would be remarkable for us to do otherwise. In saying this, I know that I risk the charge of appearing pessimistic or merely snobbish. But I speak from experience; my attempts to teach literature during the last fifteen years obviously form the basis of my judgment. I also speak with a lively memory of my own personal failures at reading. But such evidence is not the only basis for my judgment.

Let me offer a more general example: three years ago, when Robert Penn Warren's *All The King's Men* appeared, the reviews of that book, some of them written by our best-known critics and by teachers who hold distinguished posts in our better-known colleges, provided a striking instance of what I am talking about. Note that

I am not complaining at the unfavorable character of the reviews. Most of the reviews actually were favorable. And note further that I waive the whole matter of the goodness or the badness of the novel. My point is that the reviews simply made the book say things which an examination of the text would indicate the book did not say, or failed to credit the book with saying other things, and important things, which the book did say. Or, to take a more recent illustration: Faulkner's *Intruder in the Dust* was simply misread by a good many critics and reviewers as distinguished as Mr. Edmund Wilson and Miss Elizabeth Hardwick.

Now I grant that much of modern literature is difficult, though I think it ought to be borne in mind that these last illustrations have been taken from presumably the best readers that we have. But my evidence is not confined to difficult modern literature. What a good reader, including a professor of English literature, can fail to see in a poem drawn from almost any period is shocking, as I can testify from my own experience.

Yet an understanding of the literary document as a literary document is central to any valid discussion of literature. This last proposition seems to me to be an understatement. I simply do not see how we can make valuable generalizations about literature unless we can perform adequate readings of the texts on which we generalize.

Am I, then, saying that we are not to have any of the larger speculations upon literary history? Is no one to write a criticism which deals generally with the whole cultural context as it is reflected in literature? Is it not possible to try to assess the impact of certain great books upon the American consciousness? Are we not to undertake discussions of the genesis of certain great books, or to inquire how the author came to write them, or to speculate upon the general problem of how any author works? I can answer very emphatically that I hope we will have many such studies, that I think that they are legitimate fields for investigation. I certainly would not imprison the critic in a nutshell even if there, wrapped in his own speculations and in his own conceit, he might feel himself a king of infinite space.

But I point out that such studies, if they are based upon a haphazard or shoddy or biased reading of the work in question, will obviously suffer to the extent that the reading is shoddy or biased. In saying this, I do not think that I am beating a dead horse. Nearly everything that has been written on William Faulkner, for example, is stupid and irrelevant, simply because the reviewers and critics have not been able to read the novels upon which they base their generalizations. I am happy to point to honorable exceptions, including the sensible essay by Malcolm Cowley which was printed as a preface to the *Portable Faulkner* and R. P. Warren's extended review of that book. If other very considerable exceptions exist, I do not know of them, and I think that I have read nearly everything that has been written on the subject.*

To sum up, I do not think that close textual criticism, as it is sometimes scornfully called, can possibly have any quarrel with more ambitious and more general forays into criticism. It may be that too many people are engaged in writing textual criticism, though I cannot say so, in view of the general deterioration of ability to read. It may be that particular pieces of textual criticism are pedantic or wrong-

*The reader should bear in mind that this lecture was given in 1949.

headed. I have read many of them that are. One would certainly have to expect as much, human fallibility being what it is. It may be that too much textual criticism is being printed. Perhaps so. Yet I notice that the university presses still continue to groan with "objective works," some of which are excellent, but some of which learnedly document matters about as insignificant as anything that one can imagine. But I do not propose to retort for the kettle on the blackness of the pot. I would point out, however, that the shrillest catcalls as well as the most earnest exhortations for critical plain living and high thinking come from reviews sandwiched between advertisements for the bosomy "historical" novels.

What does strike me as preposterous poppycock is the silly myth which would have it that eloquent young novelists or fervid young poets are being lured away from the work to which their genius ordains them into verbal pettifogging by the wiles of a kind of wanton Acrasia called criticism. Some of them are perhaps being forced away or lured away from their proper work. I think that Hollywood may qualify for the role of enchantress, or some of our larger pulp factories, or even *The Saturday Review of Literature*. But I think that very few poets of God's making have been corrupted by this particular sorceress.

A final point. In any case, even if we decide to obey the behest of J. Donald Adams and William Rose Benet and suppress the close textual critics, or if they themselves follow Mr. Richard Chase's suggestion and commit harakiri, I hope that people who intend to generalize upon poems and novels and short stories will at least read those poems and stories and novels. I think that they might profit, in some instances, by preparing drafts of textual criticism. But I do not insist that they print them. I shall be content if they carefully but firmly place their drafts in the waste basket before they set out upon the more ambitious essay. By so doing, however, they might give us a literary history which is sound history and which is a history of *literature*, not a jumble of quotes and tips from the literary futures market or gossip from literary cocktail parties.

4 The Function of Criticism Today

THE participants in this symposium were asked to consider the function of literary criticism in America today. To the student of aesthetics the function of criticism today cannot be any different from what it was at any other period: criticism, he believes, is an ancillary discipline and its function is to elucidate the values of literature in order to improve the process of its assimilation. This was the function of criticism even in the days when the poet, the maker of literature, could count on a more coherent and better-educated audience than he does today, on one with which he was therefore capable of communicating without great loss. Even then there was the need of elucidating the poem, of clarifying its intent and revealing its values, and this was not only the reader's need but also the poet's, not because the one distrusted his creative powers and the other his taste, but because men increase their grasp of the objective content of a poem by comparing their discriminations. This is true in spite of the well-known antagonism which exists between artist and critic, for I am speaking of the function of criticism not in a descriptive but in a normative way.

But if this has always been the critic's task, why need we ask what is his function today? Yet the question is very much with us, nor was it invented by the distinguished scholars who have honored the participants of this symposium with the invitation to help them celebrate the centennial of a great institution. A very hasty reference to a number of recent articles and books is sufficient to prove how obtrusive the question is. I refer to such books as *Theory of Literature* by Wellek and Warren, to the Blackmur article, "A Burden for Critics," published in last summer's *The Hudson Review*, to Robert Stallman's anthology, to the last chapter and the first two appendixes of *The Well Wrought Urn*, to Hyman's *The Armed Vision* (although this book will have the distinction, I fear, of adding to the current confusion a number of errors which no one had the wit to think of heretofore), and also to a number of articles of polemical nature, among which, because of their challenging quality, we must not forget to include those of the Chicago School, as Trowbridge dubbed them, by Crane and Elder Olson. This activity indicates, particularly when one considers the high quality of most of it, that there exists in contemporary criticism what we have fallen into the facile custom of calling a "crisis," into whose nature and cause we need to inquire if we are to answer intelligently the question that we have been asked to consider.

My first question, then, is whether conditions have altered so radically that what aesthetics has conceived to be the function of criticism may no longer be valid.

I do not believe that the critic's function has changed. On the contrary there is more need today than there ever was of the critic's services. But cultural changes whose effects did not become glaringly obvious until the second quarter of our century have forced the critic to change his actual practice, although his end remains the same. The new situation has led him to make discoveries that are far from pleasant, since it led him not only to develop techniques of analysis that enabled him to come closer to the poem than his immediate predecessors had managed to come, but also to emphasize the value of literature as literature, and this has been taken to impinge on vested interests. The men who have fought this battle are usually referred to by the name given them by one of the leaders in the movement in what I take to be one of the first studies of their work: I mean, of course, *The New Criticism* by Ransom, published in 1941.

The day will come when students of our period will wonder why the activities of these men were ever called "new" and why they were received with such antagonism. But the day must be postponed so long as critics, on the one hand, insist that their task is to exhibit in public the adventure of their souls among the masterpieces, and as scholars, on the other, insist that the poem is anything but literature, that it is a philological or a historical document, or linguistic or phonetic material, and, outside the schools, that it is psychiatric or social evidence; in short that it is almost anything but what it is intended to be, a poem. If that day comes it will be seen that what the new criticism attempted was not a revolution but a counter-revolution, a restoration. What they have been trying to do is to keep the eye on the poem considered as a poem, for whether it is verse or novel or drama, it is the poem as poem that is the portal through which the reader must enter if literature is to perform its indispensable function, to give us knowledge of the complex aesthetic and moral structures which give substance to the world of immediacy in which we live.

What led to the development of the new criticism was the need to hasten the assimilation of the forms of literature that appeared after the first World War and the consequent re-evaluation of the history of literature that the assimilation of these new forms demanded. Works like *Ulysses* and *The Waste Land*, to mention only two among the most notorious, not only required to be explained when they first appeared even to that small reading public which was willing to yield to their impact rather than to react with anger, but they demanded new receptive capacities, the creating, as it has been called, of a new sensibility. The critics who attempted this task would not have gained the notoriety that they did had the world into which these poems made their appearance been equipped with the necessary agencies for their assimilation. And having said this, we have brought into our discussion factors some of which are not literary but social, and into which we must look if we are to understand the function of criticism today.

What the new critics found was that neither in the schools—among the erudite, as we say in Spanish—nor among the free-lance critics were there men who had the intense interest in literature as literature to render the required service. And as the new critics looked carefully about them they realized with increasing clarity that the service was needed, since the spread of literacy had meant the degradation of culture and the audience on which the creative artist counts had shrunk—a new audience having grown prodigiously which could consume nothing but middle-brow literature, although it must be granted that it consumed that with Gargantuan appetite.

But it was not only the degradation of culture which has proceeded side by side with the increase of literacy that made the new criticism necessary. There was another important factor involved for which I fear I lack an adequate term: let us call it the continued spread of "positivism," using the term in its widest, its original acceptation. It was not till after the first World War that the full impact of the social sciences and of the new psychologies made themselves felt on our social scene. A Wisconsin audience will appreciate the truth of this remark if it remembers that it was not until 1927 or 1928 that the first full-time anthropologist was appointed in this university. Now the social sciences represent unquestionably an important development of which we have great need in our modern world. We do not have enough positive knowledge to enable us to deal with the complexities of our modern world intelligently. We need to learn how to control business cycles; we need to teach an unteachable public the unspeakable price which we pay for our pride when we express it through racial prejudice; we need considerably more knowledge than we have of the sick soul of man, our own sick souls, in order to relieve us of our fears, anxieties, and our reflexive hatreds. However, the importance and potentialities of the social sciences have been interpreted by philosophic barbarians who have no firsthand acquaintance with spiritual values, who deny, indeed, the spirituality of value, and who therefore hopelessly confuse the function of science with the function of humanistic disciplines. This confusion, adding its own to other energies, has led to a radical disparagement of the faith men have always had in the value of literature. Positivism teaches that the cognitive value of literature has been replaced by the superior knowledge of man given us by the social sciences. The upshot of such positivism is the degradation of literature, as expressed by men like Max Eastman, whose *The Literary Mind* should be more often read, since it has the merit of expressing the pragmatic aesthetic bluntly and unambiguously, whereas *Art as Experience* conceals the bitter poison in a way in which it is not quite so easy to notice its lethal quality. Let me quote two passages from Eastman:

> This change in the relative estimation of the scientist and the man of letters is the most important change in social opinion that has occured in the fifty years intervening between Huxley and Belloc. It is one of the most important changes that has ever occurred anywhere. You might sum it up by saying that science, having displaced magic and religion and abstract philosophy as the source of help and guidance, is now successfully attacking "literature" (p. 11).

The same idea is repeated later in the book:

> As science extends and deepens its domain, those cases in which the soundest judgment can be rendered by a man cultivating the mere art of letters will grow steadily fewer (p. 246).

Since poetry is still with us and even within us and, after a fashion, even in the breast of a man like Eastman, what justification shall we give it? The answer is easy: poetry does not give us knowledge; it must be interpreted as experience; it gives us *vivid* experience. Thus it becomes a sort of benzedrine sulphate that wakens us after our arduous day at the laboratory. Consider this passage where Eastman points out that there is another way

> in which the poet can be intellectual—another way, perhaps, of defining "literary truth." Instead

of offering for belief ideas too unimportant or too difficult of verification to have been really established as true, literature can offer ideas not for belief but for enjoyment. Ideas, we must remember, are not only "about" experience; they are also experience, and so loved by poetic minds for their own sakes and regardless of their meaning's truth (p. 247).

This is the inevitable conclusion of a positivistic approach, the conclusion of the assumption that knowledge is exhaustively defined by Auguste Comte and his heirs and assigns, Dewey and Carnap. There is no fallacy in Eastman, granting his assumptions. His failure consists in the fact that he lacked the prophetic vision to foresee that when literature takes the path to which he assigns it, it ends in the activities of the poets of 632 A. F., the emotional engineers and the script writers of the feelies. But fortunately for humanity, the function of literature is not to rival science in supplying man with positive knowledge of the invariant relations of reality on which predictions can be grounded, although its function is indeed to give us knowledge—but not positive knowledge; it gives us wisdom.

And at this point we may return to the new criticism. Confronted with the threat to the humanistic values of which I have spoken, the task it has assigned itself is to "put the reader in possession of the work of art," to borrow a phrase from Mr. Brooks. But men who take art as seriously as the new critics do not find that to do this is an easy matter. For the task calls for exhibiting to direct experience how poetry, using the words of Blackmur, shows "what life is, and at present ... what our culture is."

I would prefer, did time allow it, to put the matter in quite a different way. But Blackmur's words will do and I am not altogether loath to sacrifice what I believe would be the closer approximation of my formulation for the sake of Blackmur's prestigious authority.

This, then, is the function of the critic today: to put the reader in possession of the work of art. However, I would be disloyal to my own insights if I did not regretfully state that a diffuse distrust of philosophical analysis leads the new critics to borrow ready-made notions about the use of art, like those obtained from I. A. Richards, without realizing that Richards in his aesthetics is a positivist committed to a subjectivistic interpretation of the aesthetic judgment and to a therapeutic, not to a cognitive, conception of the use of art.

This distrust of philosophy manifests itself in many ways, some of them explicit enough to mention here without going too far afield. Take for instance the polemic between Leavis and Wellek recently reprinted by Bentley in *The Importance of Scrutiny*. Of course Leavis is an English critic, but he is a "new critic," in the sense in which I have spoken here. Or take the remarks—to me astonishing in a man of his philosophical sophistication— made by Blackmur in the superb article already referred to. Philosophic studies, he tells us, are troublemakers and lead the critic into insoluble problems which are irrelevant to him as a critic. The critic, he goes on, should confine his interest in aesthetics to the study of

> superficial and mechanical executive techniques,
> partly in themselves, but also and mainly in re-

lation to the ulterior techniques of conceptual form and of symbolic form.

An attitude similar to this was once betrayed by T. S. Eliot when he confessed that he had never read much aesthetics. But such an attitude toward the fundamental problems of aesthetics leaves the critic at the mercy of implicit, always confused and often stultifying assumptions about his task and its limits, about the categories and methods he may employ, and about the function of art, concerning which he must be clear if he is not going to follow in the path of Kenneth Burke, who has left criticism altogether and is now trying to invent something that looks like a new science and is nothing but a confusion of psychoanalysis and watered-down sociology of knowledge controlled by idiosyncratic intuitions as to "what goes with what," as he puts it. This question has greater importance than may appear at first sight. For it seems to me that the frequent dissatisfaction which is found even among those who, like me, are partial to the new criticism arises from the fact that its exclusive concern with such elements as irony and tension and ambiguity unnecessarily limits the scope of their inquiry. These limitations I feel certain would be avoided if the new critics possessed a more comprehensive knowledge of the problems of aesthetics and approached art with a deeper and more philosophical conception of its uses.

5 Who Killed Cock Robin? Literary Values and the Academic Mind

Philo M. Buck

Is it a subject for academic pride or reproach that in so many places in America the serious study of literary values has turned as for refuge to the university? Many of our most ardent poets also are academics, professors or near professors of literature. Most of our stimulating and original critics lecture on literary criticism to university classes. All this seems most flattering, but can it not also be a symptom of an ailment whose effect on American creative literature may prove serious?

It was an English critic, not long ago, whose passing remark gave point to this question. It came as a compliment. Nowhere, he said, is the gap between the intellectual and the popular so wide today as in America. I wonder if this is true? And if it is, what bearing does this have upon our approach to the student mind when we academics come to an assessment of literary values? Are we of the academic robe in danger of adding to the confusion of literary values and adding one more reason for the tacit acceptance of a double standard, one for the chaste and self-denying intellectual mind, and a looser one for the more easy-going popular? Has the favorite indoor sport for those of us intellectually interested in aesthetics and literary criticism become the writing of essays, lectures, and treatises on the secret of poetry that only the initiated can understand? Has this in places partly replaced the approach to novel and poem for the "human awareness they promote, awareness of the possibilities of life?"

The urge has gone so far that some of us, who for more than a generation have watched the spread of the epidemic and have no doubt contributed to it, are almost ready to exclaim: "I have read a thousand books on the charm of poetry, and I thank God that I can still enjoy it." Who killed, or is doing his best to kill, Cock Robin, Hollywood or we professors of literature?

It is true, a blessed truth, that never in the past generation have more well-equipped students and a greater number of interested, able men been drawn to literary studies than in these years immediately following the second World War. Literary and aesthetic studies are today literally riding on the crest of a wave of interest for the right kind of young intellectuals. But again is this very fact not in itself evidence of a specialized interest never dreamed of when the university curriculum had no offerings like our seminar courses in the imagery of T. S. Eliot or Yeats? And is not this highly specialized interest a symptom that should make us take thought for our future? Can a person who is interested in a historical paradox not find room for the insinuation that there have been few ages like ours in which poetry has been more diligently *studied* and less widely read and appreciated? Certainly Plato today would find little reason to fear that our intellectuals were in any moral or metaphysical danger through our devotion to poetry.

The literary tradition, save for an occasional narrow lapse, has been dedicated to the communal nature of literature. Perhaps the word *communal* today has a somewhat sinister connotation, and it might be wiser to use the Aristotelian term *universal*. To be sure, it has always required an alert mind for its understanding, but even for the poorly equipped, literature—and above all poetry—had its lower levels of approach and enjoyment. It has seldom set itself squarely to drive off any light-armed reader by the experience of complete bewilderment. And it is the especial virtue of nineteenth-century poetry the world over, as of nineteenth-century fiction, and especially of that portion which we malign by the epithet Victorian, that it strove in comprehensibility to attain a universality that the nineteenth-century democratic liberals strove to attain in their political institutions. Certainly the greatest epochs of poetry were those that put up the fewest trespassing signs in its magic circle. Are we today making a highly specialized undertaking out of what was once a more common ritual? Do we not at times forget that the heart of the tradition is the "vital capacity for experience, a kind of reverent openness before life, and a marked moral intensity?" [1]

Or to put it the other way, have not the periods of poetry that have made something of a closed intellectual corporation of their poets and their critics made us conscious of a compensating danger, both for the poet and the reader? Was not the revolution that brought to an end the English metaphysical poetry of the seventeenth century, and no one today can deny its excellence, due less to the new logically ordered world of science, and the influence it gained over the creative imagination, than to the quasi-esoteric aloofness of its poetic practitioners? At best they sang only for the like-minded, and they offered little in the way of a compromise between bewilderment

[1] F. R. Leavis, *The Great Tradition* (London, 1948).

and understanding. Their reader must grasp the significance of allusion and imagery, reconcile the implied or
expressed paradox, or else—. It is, it was, a beautiful and
paying experience, the effort to understand. But one must
first pay the initiation fee and accept the full responsibility
of belonging before one is free in the guild of initiates.
And the number of trained initiates has been, and always
will be, small, and the first fervor will be followed by the
inevitable penalty of diminishing interest. The poetry that
came with the revolution of Dryden and Pope, whatever
its comparative merits, spoke for and to a larger world,
with a wider region of common experience, and employed
an idiom that admitted a wider understanding. Was not
the age of the so-called metaphysical poets one of the
narrow lapses in the tradition of poetry? Was it not a result of a sort of esoteric, aristocratic aloofness, a refusal
to go with the common herd and share the more common
idiom? And is there not the danger today that our academic
humanities are threatened with a similar danger?

The leading characteristic of contemporary scholarship
in our university curriculum has been one of growing
specialization. The danger for us in the humanities is that
we only too often have resorted to the ideals of scholarship and specialization in the very region that professes
to see human life as an organic whole. And the study of
literature, which is the imaginative exploitation and assessment of that life, tends to become a microscopic study
of the instruments, the symbols, the machinery of that
imagination. Of course we can have no quarrel with a detailed study, an analysis, say, of a canto of Dante's *In-
ferno*. I am thinking now of the beginning of the third
canto that would well repay the skill of the most expert

of psychoanalysts. And a nice thesis could be written on the wellings-up from Dante's unconscious mind that are the cause of *orrore* or *errore*—the disputed reading in the text (III, 31). All this would be quite pertinent and doubtless would have some ultimate value to Dante scholarship. But the *approach* of the humanities in literary criticism and poetry to the student mind lies in another direction. This is scholarship and specialization and in its way as limited to the qualified few as the problems in nuclear physics. This does not open the pages of the *Divine Comedy* to yet untrained students who understand little of the place of specialization and scholarship. This does not discover value in the essential experience of the poem. We cannot allow them to miss the wood for the trees.

Again the study of poetry that in its analysis requires an instrument of comment which in length often far exceeds the text of the poem seems to me to go far to defeat the end of poetry, at least for the average and yet unfulfilled student. It is like having to listen to the garrulous cicerone, as one stands for the first time before the campanile of San Marco, as he describes the tower, stone by stone, and how each gives its all to the larger life of the whole. One can excite curiosity this way, but one does not open the door to large and sympathetic understanding.

True, modern poetry does use "the precise word, the arresting simile, the casual but penetrating analogy." It advances by paradox—nothing new in poetry, only a more consciously used poetic device. It is true that most contemporary poets of the first rank use allusion, and often allusion remote for the average reader. And all this contributes to an ambiguity and obscurity that for some readers is as inscrutable as the quantum theory in physics, and like it available only to the eye and imagination of the specialist. And the literary criticism that grapples with such remote poetry often does small service to our unspecialized reader. Often it has its own peculiar variety of jargon, patterned on this or that science. At the conclusion of the reading of poet, critic, and comment, many a well-disposed but poor reader feels himself set off at two removes from the reality of the poetic experience, tangled now in the imagery and the explication of both poet and critic. His second state is perhaps worse than his first, with comment and criticism not breaking seals or opening vistas, but heaping discouragement on bafflement.

And this problem is made yet more difficult by the patent fact that so much of our best contemporary poetry does not offer different levels of approach for readers of varied qualification. There is little room for compromise between poet and reader, but only the remorseless alternative. The reader either reads and ponders, until he understands and enjoys, or lays the work aside with a frown of complete bewilderment. And there are times, not infrequent, when the mental process of understanding is not wholly unlike the almost purely intellectual labor of following a complicated experiment in chemistry. How can we disassociate the more narrow and intellectual outlook of such specialized scholarship from the broad horizon of the humanities?

The malady, if it be a malady, or the blessing, if the contrary be true, is seen in its most acute or beneficent view in the small closed companies, like joint stock corporations, of the devoted followers of the Muses. They are on every campus, and, bless them, they need both our admiration and sympathy. Devoted to the propagation of

light, as they have seen the light and follow the gleam;
seeking with the devotion of saints—and I am not jesting
—to make known the mission of the "new poetry," but
the true significance of whose mission they do not quite
understand—except that it is for the elect and initiate,
and that for the crass multitude it is an arcanum, they
dream in terms of a new campus poetry magazine, and of
the virtues of paper and printer's ink, and of the mystery
of a new poetic image that shall communicate, only to the
elect, the ineffable last poetic experience. Where is the
difference between their unselfish devotion and that of
the brotherhood of future Einsteins who dream of a new
mathematics and the last mystery of atom or galaxy laid
bare for their corporate and specialized understanding,
but to the uninitiate a pious secret.

I think we are all agreed that the ideal in a study of
literature and in all that we try to do in literary criticism
is to open up new ideas and ways of life and attitudes for
the intelligent imagination of the students, philosophies
of life in the concrete. Is not this ambition after all the
most precious motive for all that we call the study of the
humanities? Do many of our best-known new poets, do
our specialized studies of poetry in our specialized universities aid the humanities in this most essential service? In
this day it is so easy for the youthful student, whose
heritage is enthusiasm for some ideal beyond himself, to
find himself astray in some dark wood of cynical disillu-
sionment. So many, and their numbers are startling, for
I speak from painful experience, are looking for "a way,"
and we offer them specialized scholarship. They want enthusiasm and inspiration—I use these words in their ety-

mological meaning—and we offer them a mental cross-
word puzzle.

A personal illusion will, I am sure, stir the memory of
all of us. If there is one experience in my own college
days which more than any other was the voice of a Vergil
to a lost wanderer in a dark wood, it was of a professor
of Greek once reading aloud to a small class the moving
lines of the chorus in Aeschylus' *Persians*. The words were
Greek and Greek to most of us, but not his voice or expression. As the tears coursed down his bearded cheeks
some of us learned—it was a vision—that the rhythms
and images of Aeschylus were not an exercise in specialized philology, but human poetry and passion. That day
we read no farther.

In the meanwhile Hollywood goes on catering as usual
to the universal and not to the highly specialized interests
of Americans and others. To be sure, the level is low, and
we are only too free in our criticism of the debauchery
of American taste. They spread still wider the gap between
the intellectual and the popular; but who of us dare
to cast a stone? For if their sin against the tradition of
art and poetry is grievous, is ours any the less deadly
in our pharisaical aloofness. If they kill by the surfeit
of the less than humanly intellectual, do we not also
often bring death by leading our followers into the desert
where the waterholes are only too infrequent? And again
as at the beginning—who kills Cock Robin, the Academe
or Hollywood?

What has all this to do with the subject of literary
criticism? The answer is, everything. For it is impossible,
at any time, to separate the twin sisters, Literature, the

elder, and Literary Criticism, the ministering junior. The younger sister, consciously or unconsciously, never leaves the side of the elder. What every alert defender of the tradition of the humanities should never forget is that our elementary courses in literature, as well as the more specialized studies, deeply concern questions of human life and human conduct and are not chiefly interesting opportunities to exploit the sum of human knowledge. The question, yes, the moral question, of human value will always be the most important for every literary critic. It is also the one to which every student as anxiously is looking for an answer. May I conclude with a sentence from W. H. Auden, who is poet first and critic after. He has mentioned the two problems for the critic, that of communication and that of value. Where shall we look for value, he argues, save in the excellence of the human tradition. For "when tradition disappears so does popular taste."

6 Historical and Humanistic Values

Howard Mumford Jones

Let me begin by avoiding a simple confusion. It may be expected that one who represents the arts, or at any rate the art of literature, might take his stand in this discussion on the simple proposition that, whatever else it may be, history is itself an art. It is not history until it is written, and, as my neighbor, Mr. Bernard De Voto, goes on to say, it is not history until it is read. With Mr. De Voto's indictment of history as unreadable except in academic circles, one may have a good deal of sympathy, just as one may have a good deal of sympathy with his thesis that, precisely because he was an artist, Francis Parkman is probably the greatest American historian. But to reopen this ancient dispute from the side of literary values would get us nowhere. My instructions as to the part I am supposed to play in this symposium were, by reason of time and distance, inevitably hazy, but I have, I hope rightly, inferred that whatever else I might contribute, that something was not to reopen the problem of historiography. In truth I sometimes think there are as many theories of history as there are practicing historians; and even when you confine yourself to the smaller area of literary history, you can find almost any sort of theoretical approach, just as you can find books written under theories so faint that they virtually present no theory at all. The search for a new and universal theory of historical writing occasionally brings us new insights and fresh values, but in my observation, unless theoretical novelty is coupled with that general good sense which it is the business of humanistic study to mature, discussions of theory are more productive of disputes than they are of determinations.

Let me talk, then, about the history of the arts, that is, of the fine arts, since I am a practitioner of one branch of this division of history; namely, the history of literature.

So far as the history of the arts is concerned, I suggest that a history of the arts—almost any history of the arts, and almost any historical approach to any art—seems to oscillate between two poles. At the one extreme is the doctrine that any work of art, no matter where or when or by whom it was produced, immediately expresses itself and only itself, so that historical inquiry is both misleading and superfluous. And in some sense this is true. Anybody looking at the statues brought to the British Museum from Easter Island has an immediate impression of weight and mass and clumsy power of delineation. Similarly, in Emerson's phrase, the schoolboy in the corner reading Shakespeare need know nothing of Plantagenet England, Tudor kings, or Renaissance man to get from the plays something immediate, stimulating, and unique. It neither increases nor diminishes the beauty of sound in the overture to *Don Giovanni* to know that it was written under the stimulus of punch and funny stories only two nights before the first production. This is one end of the spectrum—the theory that the history of an art has so little to do with artistic meaning as to be superfluous.

The other extreme is more difficult to present without absurdity, but it is either the assumption that no comprehension of the work of art is possible except in an historical matrix or the assumption that the chief value of the work is not as art but as artifact, that is, as documentary evidence toward a state of culture. There was once a celebrated year-long course in the works of Edmund Spenser taught at a university not a thousand miles from here; and the scholar in charge was, according to legend, so concerned to lay a firm historical foundation for the poet's work that the class got around to *The Faerie Queene* only in the last two weeks of the last term. The professor justified this procedure by saying that they could read *The Faerie Queene* any time, since they would now understand it as they were incapable of understanding it before. If the story is not true, it is at least well invented. A more ordinary example is those passages in *The Rise of American Civilization* in which the Beards paid their devoir to writing in America, writers and books being classified into an intelligible historical framework without much pretense at aesthetic comment. Inadequate as this treatment is, neither music nor the arts of design nor the arts of the theater received even this much attention from these leading historians.

Good sense, it seems to me, avoids both extremes. The absurdity of the Spenser course is patent, and the inadequacy of the account of American writers in the Beards' history is evident. Less evident is the absurdity of that aesthetic theory which stoutly refuses to be contaminated by historical information. It is, however, scarcely true that the quintessential meaning of a work of art is something out of space, out of time; and it is a remarkable commentary on the doctrine that its enunciation by Croce is now something that has to be looked up and considered historically. In truth, it is virtually impossible to avoid significant historical reference even in the case of masterpieces. As soon as you have said "Don Giovanni," you have, by merely thinking the words, brought into the mind, unless you are innocent of any culture whatsoever, a whole train of associations about Spanish legend, about Mozart, about eighteenth-century music—information which is, as it were, so common that it takes no special act of the will to accept these implications, whereas it would take a self-conscious and virtually impossible act of the will to avoid them. Or take, if you prefer, the tragedy of *Romeo and Juliet*. It is a story of star-crossed lovers, valid and persuasive by right of its own poetry. So, too, the story of Pyramus and Thisbe is, or once was, valid and persuasive. But nobody in his senses has ever supposed that these poems were written simultaneously by the same sort of genius in the same sort of culture. One is obviously Renaissance English; one is obviously Latin culture of the Augustan age. But as soon as you have said this, you have admitted history, for these cultural terms are rich in historical overtones which you cannot silence if you will.

What, then, has history to do with the arts? How does it oscillate between these extremes? What humanistic value is involved?

It may momentarily confuse the issue, but it will not in the long run confuse the issue, if I say that the historical problem is not the same in all the arts. Allowing for the ravages of time, artifacts produced in the visual arts remain relatively constant until they disappear. The statue, the painting, the building, the engraving do not essentially alter except as time crumbles or darkens them. You can look at Michelangelo's "David" and you will see the identical stone that Renaissance man saw, though you may not see it the same way or see all the details or values he beheld. Yet there is a rough persistency, a constancy in such works; otherwise iconology and iconography would have a pretty tough time of it. On the other hand, the dance leaves no permanent record behind it—at least, did not until the invention of the motion picture. Between these two extremes are arts like music, drama, and literature. In the case of music, at least in modern times, there are musical scores, but the farther back you go in time, into the Middle Ages or the music of the ancient world, the score vanishes, and you get into highly disputable territory where some people read neumes one way and some another, and so on. In arts employing language, however—literature, oratory, the theater—the verbal signs (like the musical signs) remain constant, but the meaning is likely to alter with the lapse of ages. One simple instance from a nonliterary document in English is worth a thousand more complex examples: the founding fathers wrote the so-called "commerce" clause into the American Constitution, but they would be utterly bewildered, could they return to this industrial age and discover what the Supreme Court has made of this simple mercantile noun. So likewise neither Aristophanes nor Mark Twain is now as funny as once they were, for when you have to explain a joke, the joke usually vanishes.

It seems to me, in the light of these considerations, that the task of the historian in the field of the arts is a double one. He discovers, or is told, that certain artistic performances were important in a given culture in their own time, a fact for which there is documentary or other evidence; or he discovers, or is told, that certain artistic performances which perhaps did not seem originally, to him or to those living in the historical culture, significant are, in the light of subsequent developments, important— to subsequent cultures or even to contemporary culture. In either case his duty is, as it were, through an act of the historical imagination based on scholarship, to reconstruct the matrix in which the performance was originally embedded, and in the light of this reconstruction to help us to understand what the original conditions, the original purpose, and the original success of the work must have been. The exact quantum of technical skill required of him for this task will obviously vary with the nature of the art and with the nature of the particular task; and if he is a general historian he may be poorly equipped to deal with all the arts. But if he is an historian of a particular art, it goes without saying that he ought to have the proper technical facility.

But this is, I think, only half of his duty, and it is the second half of his task that arouses debate. For, except as antiquarianism has its charm, the modern reader still has the right to ask the historian: whatever the importance of this artifact, this literary composition, this music a thousand or ten thousand years ago, why is it of any importance to *me*? The historian's duty is then also, it seems to me, to account for the *continuing* importance of the work into our day.

This he may do in several ways. He may appeal to universal consent. For example, it is scarcely necessary to convince modern readers that Sophocles was and continues to be a great tragic poet. Or he may appeal to the judgment of experts, of connoisseurs, of informed persons. A case in point would be some of the abstruser reaches of musicology, or a discussion of the metrical system of Arabic verse. Or he may, of course, simply announce on his own responsibility the discovery of a neglected work of genius, though in my observation this sort of thing is likely in the long run to be disastrous more times than not.

In any case, the historian of an art requires, as I have said, sufficient technical knowledge to know what he is talking about, and he ought to have enough general sympathy and critical insight—and I am using the term loosely—so that he does not substitute the work of one period or place for that of another, or mistake meretricious production for first-class achievement. But this, surely, is sufficient. I do not think it is his primary duty to be a critic in the same sense that one thinks of Coleridge or Walter Pater or Sainte-Beuve or Goethe as critics. I think he may avail himself of any insights that aesthetic criticism has to offer, but I would still suggest that his primary duty is to explain, as justly as he can, not so much the aesthetic value of a work of art as its importance in the history of human culture. If he will but cling to this idea he will, it seems to me, avoid that sterile antiquarianism of which aesthetic criticism justly complains, and he will not get entangled in the critical disputatiousness of his own time. For if he does become so entangled, his own work will fade away in proportion as the dispute fades away, precisely as nineteenth-century political historians who tried to read the past in terms of Whig or Tory triumph have faded. He will, by remaining a historian, help the critic to acquire a juster sense of proportion in time and taste, and he will help the reader to keep contemporary criticism in due temporal perspective by reminding that reader how ephemeral dogma enunciated as eternal truth by criticism in the past has usually turned out to be. And he will aid the political historian by quietly insisting that politics is not, like conduct, three-fourths of life, and that the ideals and values of the human species are as often embodied in the statues of their gods and the songs of their poets as they are embodied in government or forms of warfare. In sum, in the fine arts the historian, ideally considered, ought to perform a mediatorial function, constantly reminding us of the relativity of our prejudices in matters of beauty by compelling us to consider that other men and other cultures have been at least as happy as are we in creating forms of art satisfactory to themselves and of some importance to others.

7 The Centrality of Humanistic Study

Nathan M. Pusey

It has been my observation, based, to be sure, on familiarity with only a few institutions of higher learning, and perhaps for too short a time, that there is some reason for considering a university to be less a community of scholars engaged in harmonious and cooperative search for truth than a frenetic aggregate of jealous partisans. The members of a university faculty live together, but not infrequently, it appears, on terms rather of mutual sufferance than of community and high respect. Their association, outwardly showing a semblance of politeness and amity, may inwardly be marred by suspicions and distrust, even by contempt, one for another.

I am sure, if we are honest, that all of us who belong to the trade can only smile wryly when we hear the word "community" applied to anything as atomistic as a college or university faculty. For the fact seems to be that members of faculties as a rule are less concerned to work amiably and selflessly with their colleagues in other disciplines than to assert the pre-eminent and superior worth of their own, and to establish and magnify its merits by belittling the less important, perhaps even faintly ridiculous, fields of study that somehow earlier caught the eccentric interests and mediocre talents of their less able colleagues.

So do we all feel more important in the world and achieve apparently some kind of necessary catharsis. It is in such a spirit of partisanship, quite frankly, that I wish to speak today—as a partisan primarily of the liberal arts curriculum, but within this, more especially of the humanities (in which classification I include history)—and to make my case I will first, following the professional practice I have just deplored, speak *against* two other kinds of intellectual activity.

But perhaps this is not too bad, for the areas of knowledge the handling of which I should like to criticize are those least in need of apologetic treatment at the present time, namely, the natural and the social sciences. The relevance of their subject matters to present-day life is obvious to almost everyone, and their attainments—cumulative, multiform, impressive—beyond the reach of faultfinding. And I would point out circumspectly that I have no quarrel with the importance of either of these fields of study or with their achievements. I am not that benighted or irresponsible. But I do want to say something critical concerning the educational value of these disciplines as recently, and even in some places currently, practiced.

The partisans of the natural sciences rightly urge the importance to higher education of the body of knowledge which is theirs to keep alive, augment, and teach, and emphasize the importance of some familiarity with and understanding of the physical world to every one of us. It is impossible for me to see how anyone could object to this. The need for such knowledge is beyond dispute. But when they go further and make claims concerning the by-products which come with the acquisition of the knowledge, *i.e.*, when they set out to insist upon the peculiar and necessary importance of their studies in producing certain traits of mind and sets of character (and these claims are made again and again), I confess that it is here that experience has made me frankly skeptical. I wish that all the claims of this kind that I have heard were true, but I just do not think they are.

Teachers of science in their apologetic literature are likely to say, for example, that the study of their subjects, experience in their disciplines, is of indispensable value in teaching people to think effectively and in inculcating certain desirable traits of mind. Their studies, it is claimed, will teach people, if anything can, to see and observe; to examine data; to analyze, weigh, measure; to withhold judgment; to think precisely, exactly, carefully from observed facts; to observe general principles and relationships, to formulate tentative explanations and to test them. They also teach habits of industry and fortitude, and, mounting higher, it is maintained that such studies engender a love for truth and respect for evidence. They teach young people to put aside their personal feelings and all other irrelevant considerations, to look at facts or at least at certain ranges of fact and to take the broad, impersonal, objective, honest, scientific view of them.

This is where my question comes, for I do not think they do. That is, I do not think the study of the sciences as widely practiced in the last generation, and at some places even now, does accomplish these things. I cannot speak of how the person trained largely, if not exclusively, on a diet of science behaves at work within his own field: I am willing to admit that he practices all these virtues there, for I cannot check him. But if the study of science did pre-eminently produce these very desirable traits of mind, one could reasonably expect to find them most conspicuously displayed in general discussion by individuals who had been longest engaged in the study of courses in science, let us say, by their teachers. And it would follow that on college and university faculties the teachers of science, as a class, could therefore be counted on especially for intellectual curiosity, for objectivity and a passion for truth wherever it leads, for humility and freedom from the desire for personal triumph. And I offer it as one man's opinion that this simply is not so. The point that I want to make now is that there is much evidence, if we look at the behavior of teachers of science outside their laboratories, as compared with that of other teachers, to suggest that courses in science by themselves are patently inadequate to produce the educational results commonly claimed for them. And a similar indictment, if this word is admissible, can be brought on the record against any similar claims that may be put forth by teachers of social science. Again let me say there can be no reservations concerning the importance of their subject matters nor with their earnest and commendable aim of understanding modern society in all its ramifications with a view to improving human relationships (though we may perhaps have some reservations concerning their too ready proclivity for the hortatory mood). The only quarrel I wish to make is with any claim made for their study to an exclusive, or even to a primary, value in developing certain desirable intellectual qualities, among which are respect for fact, objectivity, initial withholding of judgment, and finally, judgment in accord with and in proportion to the evidence. Again it is my claim, supported by such observations as I have been able to make in the educational world, that the social studies, when tested by the general intellectual behavior of their teachers outside their field, can no more be relied upon to insure critical, unbiased, impersonal reflections and imaginative thinking than can the natural sciences.

The point of this paper is simply to present the testimony of one individual who has worked with teachers from various disciplines in several institutions of higher learning, and who has had an opportunity of observing those in a number more, that if there is any generalization possible concerning the acquisition of desirable mental qualities from the study of particular subject matters—and I am not sure that there is—then it is that the humanities, concerned primarily with the conduct, the behavior, the aspirations and achievements, the reasons and rationalizations of individual human beings as recorded and preserved by our artists, are more apt than either of the other major areas of the curriculum to give them, even (and this is where my statement will seem most incredible to some), even and especially those virtues which we generally assume to characterize the scientific mentality—humility, accuracy, judgment in proportion to the facts.

"By their fruits ye shall know them." I have in my way tried continually to apply this test, and I find that the case for the humanities becomes clearer and clearer. I find, ironically and curiously, that those qualities of mind thought to accrue from the study of the sciences are most likely to be found in teachers of the sciences in proportion to their experience in other than their own disciplines.

The educated man and the man of judgment will ignore any of the chief divisions of knowledge to his cost, but it would almost seem that lack of experience with the humanities can be virtually fatal. This is the testimony I offer for what it is worth.

It is an initial and indispensable, if not exclusive, function of higher education not merely to impart knowledge, but in doing this, to transform personality by transforming minds. It is an essential aim of education to call into quickened responsiveness the recalcitrant, darkened, and confused learning apparatus—imaginative, mental, emotional—with which we are each endowed. Our natural minds need to be transformed and developed, but they can be neither transformed nor developed by the mere passage of time, or merely by uninspired exercise, or by materials that do not speak directly to the human soul. True mental growth, it seems, can come only from contact with great and original ideas as they have operated in the minds of exceptional individuals and from vivid experience with exceptionally meaningful bits of human experience.

Every human being needs direct personal contact with the great stories, myths, and fictions of the human race, and with history, to begin to know himself and to sense the potentialities—of all sorts, for good and for bad—that lie within his reach and the reach of other men. The reaches of the human soul and the distortions the human mind is capable of, the meanness that often mars our judgments and the great liberations we can achieve, what it is to be a man and what it can be, these things are known through the lives and actions of individuals who speak to us by means of art and in the pages of history. Not the scientific exploration of things, not the scientific examination of the behavior of groups of people, but the living, vivid acquaintance with the adventures of the human spirit, this it is which especially can stretch the humanity that lies in a man from birth and needle it into its fullest growth.

But the curious fact is that it is also this experience, this imaginative acquaintance with what I. A. Richards so aptly called our "storehouse of recorded values," that seems to be most efficacious in producing those qualities of mind which we feel are essential to the scientific way of doing things, the way our world so desperately needs today. He who has followed man's story in history and who has lived long with the great fictions men have produced, whether he be scientist, social scientist, or some other, can be relied on, if anyone can, for humaneness, for temperate judgment, for respect for fact, for awareness of kinds of facts, for objectivity and judiciousness, and for concern.

A man can live, we may suppose, though not very well or very long, without an extensive acquaintance with the natural sciences. He could probably get on, though as a group we shall certainly not get ahead, without much experience in the social sciences. But he cannot be a good natural scientist or social scientist without first being a fully developed man, and he will not be that if he is not acquainted, richly acquainted, with humanistic studies.

I hope it will not destroy the effect of what I have said if I now add that in my opinion both the natural and social sciences can be and should be made a part of the humanistic studies. But they will be so incorporated only as they are cultivated by men who have worked also in the narrower field which we call the humanities, including history.

It is often argued that philosophy or religion should

permeate every department of a curriculum, and I think there is much to be said to support this view. But in the same way I feel that literary and historical studies should affect the minds and hearts and emotions of everyone working in any branch of knowledge, for he will function to the best advantage both public and private wherever he is, of this I am convinced, only as he has been awakened and disciplined by the quickening, transforming, and perfecting power of humanistic study.

Many years ago Matthew Arnold, speaking in this country, closed a discussion of this subject with these words:

> While we shall all have to acquaint ourselves with the great results reached by modern science, and to give ourselves as much training in its disciplines as we can conveniently carry, yet the majority of men will always require humane letters; and so much the more, as they have the more and the greater results of science to relate to the need in man for conduct, and to the need in him for beauty.

The years that have elapsed since seem only to have underscored the truth of this early observation.

8 The Special Significance of the Humanities in Liberal Education

Clark G. Kuebler

IT HAS become uncomfortably clear that the world is in the throes of an ideological war, a war of which World War II was only another phase. We are battling over ideas and ideals; and, as we battle, we realize more and more that what a man believes in, he is and does. "Character is destiny."

In fighting for democracy as opposed to totalitarianism in any form, we are involved in a struggle which is only superficially one of politics and economics; fundamentally, it is one of values. And, ironically, the values believed in by the totalitarians are all too clear, while the values held to by believers in democracy are often all too vague. Furthermore, since space-destroying machinery has made it possible to disseminate ideas and ideals as never before, for us to be vague and our enemies to be definite in their idealism is a terrifyingly serious problem, perhaps more serious than at any time in the history of the Western World.

Why do we of the democracies find ourselves confused as to human values? Why are we unable to oppose to the crude, naturalistic aims of the totalitarians aims which are clear, affirmative, and compelling? For half a century our civilization has been preoccupied with science and technology; and the result has been an alarming tendency to mechanical materialism, to a naïve assumption that science and technology are sufficient for the development of a good society. The experience of the last two decades should have made indubitable the fact that machines can either advance or destroy civilization, depending entirely upon what ends they serve; and, unfortunately, we have been more concerned with means than with ends, or with what is most valuable in human life.

Because of the overwhelming authority of science and the scientific method, many modern educators have virtually shoved aside the humanities. Too many have been worshipping the logical process and have known only an external world and social phenomena. To those central experiences of value which condition personality and give life meaning, modern man has given his attention hardly at all. In short, the humanities, which are primarily concerned with values and their critical appraisal, have been seriously neglected or, at best, underemphasized.

Since the content of the humanities is man's experience of value, his purposes, and his standards, they are concerned with what is most intimately and inherently human. Furthermore, according to Ralph Barton Perry, they embrace whatever influences conduce to the essential freedom of man. In fact, the humanities are inextricably bound up with man's freedom, because freedom is possible only when man can make enlightened choices; and enlightened choices involve not merely reflexes or habits, but reflection and fundamental insights into what is good and bad and what is the will of God. A student of the humanities apprehends, analyzes, and interprets expressed insights into the values which are to be found in art, literature, ethics, and religion. And, when philosophy and history reveal these insights, they, too, are classified in the humanistic discipline as enabling man to make considered choices in the realm of value.

For the past few decades serious harm has been done by overemphasizing the so-called scientific method in the teaching of the humanities. Literature has been dissected and treated like a biological specimen. The error has been one of failing to recognize that fact and value lie in different realms and that, although both are real, each calls for different methods of examination and appraisal. In the humanities the approach to reality, unlike that in the pure sciences, is essentially one of evaluation rather than measurement; the concern is with the significance of the subject matter for man as man, not in any restricted sense, but for the whole man of physics and metaphysics. And the humanities are concerned, moreover, with man's perfectibility. In other words, they deal with man not only in a descriptive or an apologetic sense, but eulogistically—man in his greatest and highest capacity. For that reason the approach to reality is not impersonal and dispassionate as it is in the sciences; but both these approaches to reality are real and necessary. Precisely because that is true, the humanities furnish the most effective vehicle man can use in apprehending and communicating that which gives human experience its special significance.

The greatest single obstacle to man's enlarging his sense of ultimate values is the excessive specialization which characterizes present-day civilization. Bergson has pointed out that the chief characteristic of the lower animals is specialization *ad infinitum*; in contrast to a human being, a beast does one thing admirably, but only one thing. Clearly the evils of excessive specialization do not call for abandoning specialization; *abusus non tollit usum*. The remedy is a synthesis, a fusion of particulars, a redefinition of man's true destiny and a rediscovery of his larger cultural heritage. Such wisdom is the goal of all humanistic study.

Finally, the humanities are particularly necessary in any truly liberalizing educational experience because the freedom of thought and the responsible action which make up the very stuff of human dignity are being threatened increasingly by industrial, political, and militaristic mechanization. As we stress the need for the humanities in our fight against present tyrannies, we must remember always that humanistic endeavor is as lasting as life itself and has been integral to human dignity in every age and every civilization.

9 Humanism in Science

Henry Guerlac

T HERE has never been a period of modern history when
what we commonly call science—meaning, of course, the
natural sciences—has not struck many persons as the antithesis, perhaps even the enemy, of what we loosely lump
together as the humanities. Two popular stereotypes about
science have contributed to the prevalence of this attitude.
The first, which we can call the Gradgrind theory, always
assumes that the scientist deals only with facts, usually
qualified for some reason as "stubborn" or "brute" facts,
which it is his sordid custom to transform into columns of
figures or express in unaesthetic graphs and charts. According to this theory, science is hopelessly materialistic and
deals mainly with dull, prosaic matters, a failing which is
excusable when the studies prove useful to us, but which
seems absurd when we cannot detect any practical purpose
beyond the innocent amusement of the investigator. The
second view is not much more favorable, though it is more
sophisticated; for it recognizes that science deals in reality
more with ideas about things than with things themselves.
This view complains that although scientific inquiry is a
search for truth, it is often too abstract and too mathema-
matical to be really in touch with human life and man's
individual and social problems. Here again science and the
humanities seem to have lost all contact: for science is concerned with the barren wastes of inanimate nature, if not
its mathematical shadowland, while the humanities deal
with the rich and varied spectrum of human experience.

Of course these are both caricatures, which is a very good reason why they are likely to have both a wide currency and a considerable life expectancy. The two opinions, it should be noted, have one thing in common, though they approach the problem from opposite sides: both assume that either science is indifferent to man's peculiarly human problems, or it is concerned only with providing inordinately, with a never ceasing flow of goods, for his animal needs and socially created desires.

Let us ask how far these criticisms are justified and inquire to what degree science—especially in the seventeenth and early eighteenth centuries, the age when it first became aware of its separate identity and was struggling to formulate its ideals and its goals—did in fact tend to exclude or indefinitely postpone the study of man. Did its methods or attitudes inevitably lead to ignoring human values, and could it have been at the same time grossly materialistic, unduly remote from reality, and wholly indifferent to man's fate?

That scientific discovery is a complex human activity was already apparent by the end of the seventeenth century, when the two tendencies I have mentioned had clearly revealed themselves and were already being ridiculed. Thomas Sprat, the historian of the Royal Society, lamented in 1667 that the experimenters of the Society, called in the language of the day the *virtuosi*, were criticized by some for aiming too high and by others for aiming too low. The adversaries and worldy critics of what was styled the New Experimental Learning found its interests to be at once too vulgar and too abstract and lampooned it unmercifully on both counts. In his satirical comedy *The Virtuoso*, Shadwell poked coarse fun at the

investigators to whom nothing was too revolting to be
painstakingly studied.[1] The protagonist, Sir Nicholas Gimcrack, "the finest speculative gentlemen in the whole
world," is disrespectfully described by one of his nieces,
Clarinda, as "A sot, that has spent 2000 pounds in Micro-
scopes, to find out the nature of Eels in Vinegar, Mites in
Cheese, and the blue of Plums, which he has subtilly found
out to be living creatures." Dean Swift in his description
of the Academy of Lagado did not overlook this weakness,
but his sharpest barbs were reserved for the opposite tendency when he conjures up the absent-minded, im-
practical, and easily deceived mathematicians of Gulliver's
floating island of Laputa, "in the common actions and behavior of life . . . a clumsy, awkward, unhandy people."

There is some justice in these criticisms, even though
they are criticisms of extremes; for they point to tendencies
in science to which some men, some times, some scientific
fashions have shown great partiality. It must be confessed
that both Shadwell and Swift struck home with deadly
accuracy, and the often uncritical, acquisitive, bumbling
Baconian curiosity of the early Royal Society is well taken
off in Sir Nicholas Gimcrack. Yet the other tendency was
equally evident; for at the same time—with all its talk of
observation and experiment—the ideal of science in the
seventeenth century (only think of the names of Descartes,
John Wallis, Newton, and Huygens) was mathematical,
Archimedean.

An emphasis on mathematical formalism, by a para-
doxical and unholy alliance with the hypothesis of materialism, was daily bringing successes that staggered the

[1] Claude Lloyd, "Shadwell and the Virtuosi," in *Publications of the
Modern Language Association*, 44:472–494 (1929).

imagination. These great triumphs effectively banished spiritual forces and final causes from the domain of physics and from the serious consideration of scientists. To the distress of the conservative, the occult qualities, the substantial forms, and the other semantic traps of the scholastic imagination were relegated to the boneyard. With the air thus cleared, the mechanical philosophy was applied with heady optimism on every hand; the physical world seemed to be a complex engine, a great clock of innumerable moving material parts; much that was thought to be part and parcel of this world proved on closer examination to be only our own subjective evaluation of it. By denying the objective reality of everything in nature except matter in motion, and excluding everything that could not be spatially or temporally measured, the new physics of Galileo, Descartes, Boyle, and Newton reduced the scientific importance of the so-called "secondary qualities" (color, sound, odor, the sensations of heat and cold)—all that gave color, meaning, and richness to ordinary life.

Prematurely and at greater peril, these mechanical ideas were introduced into the realm of biology: a school of physicians called the iatrophysicists tried to explain all bodily functions and disarrangements on purely mechanical terms. Giovanni Borelli, a disciple of Galileo, carried out a classic analysis of muscular and skeletal motion in the human body in terms of simple machines and explained locomotion, respiration, and digestion as purely mechanical processes.

A more extreme member of this school was Giorgio Baglivi (1668–1705), a pupil of the great anatomist Malpighi, who conceived the bodily machine as itself an assemblage of smaller machines and compared the teeth to scissors, the stomach to a flask, the heart and blood vessels—as Harvey had done—to a system of water works, the thorax to a pair of bellows. The more complicated bodily processes were rashly explained, by men like Baglivi, in terms of the fine structure of fibers, glands, ducts, and secretions which the earliest microscopic examinations had made evident. Physiological theories of this sort had an immense vogue and a very considerable influence in the early eighteenth century.

These were indeed crude attempts, which lent support to the opinion that the mechanical philosophy was crude and naïve. But to the the physicist, be it said, there was nothing "crass" about matter. Its behavior might be followed, but its nature and essence were forever hidden. Still more remarkable, it proved quite unnecessary—and perhaps neither desirable nor possible—to describe nature only in its tangled and varying complexity. Galileo, the most amazing genius of this surprising century, had shown how fruitful it could be to account for the behavior of the real world in terms of ideal mechanisms, of material systems that existed in full perfection only in his own mind: a world of perfect spheres, frictionless surfaces, empty space, and unceasing motions. It was this, by the way, that made possible the fullest extention of the concept of *scientific law*, in many ways the greatest achievement of the first scientific century. But men often forgot to caution others, or did not themselves fully realize, that these simple mathematical rules that nature apparently followed, and which exhibited the mathematical elegance with which God seemed to have planned the physical universe, were in fact the absolute laws of only an imaginary, ideal, nonexistent Platonic world of the Galilean imagination.

Here we have it! On the one hand the casual botanizing, the passionate curiosity, the moth-eaten specimens, the fetal monsters, and all the crowded dusty disorder of the virtuoso's cabinet; and on the other, a mathematical fairyland, floating above the earth like Gulliver's island. If either or both together exhaust the content of science, then surely humanism, by any definition, suggests a richer diet, and something nobler and closer to man's real interests. But you sense, I am sure, that these are the same caricatures with which I began, portraits of two quite familiar but opposing tendencies in science. With no intention of pushing the comparison too far, my caricatures, I think, correspond to the division of scientific temperaments into the classic and romantic types long ago proposed by the chemist Wilhelm Ostwald. With good effect, William Morton Wheeler, the grand old Harvard entomologist, while admitting that most scientists of his acquaintance were a mixture of these two tendencies, applied this classification in order to contrast the laboratory biologist with the more desultory naturalist:

> The naturalist is mentally oriented toward and controlled by objective, concrete reality, and probably because his senses, especially those of sight and touch, are highly developed, is powerfully affected by the esthetic appeal of natural objects. He is little interested in and may even be quite blind to abstract or theoretical considerations. . . . When philosophically inclined, he is apt to be a tough-minded Aristotelian. . . .
>
> The biologist *sensu stricto*, on the other hand, is oriented toward and dominated by ideas, and

rather terrified by or oppressed by the intricate hurly-burly of concrete, sensuous reality and its multiform and multicolored individual manifestations. He often belongs to the motor rather than to the visual type and obtains his esthetic satisfaction from all kinds of analytical procedures and the cold desiccated beauty of logical and mathematical demonstration. . . . He is a denizen of the laboratory. His besetting sin is oversimplification and the tendency to undue isolation of the organisms he studies from their natural environment. As a philosopher he is apt to be a tender-minded Platonist. . . .[2]

Perhaps it is significant that the terms for these extreme tendencies in science have been borrowed from what I take to be extreme tendencies in literature, music, and art, which is quite proper, since the taxonomy of scientific history is far less rich than the historical vocabulary of the humanities. I hope I shall not seem impertinent—and I am certainly in no danger of being original—if I suggest that the taxonomy of literary history—like all taxonomy, for that matter—is based on the easily characterized extremes, and that the words "classic" and "romantic" no more describe suitably the greatest figures of literature and art and music than they do those of science, however well they may serve to lump together the lesser men. The classic and

[2] Quoted in Charles P. Curtis, Jr. and Ferris Greenslet, *The Practical Cogitator or the Thinker's Anthology* (Boston, 1945), pp. 207–208. The original appeared in William Norton Wheeler's "What is Natural History?" in *Bulletin of the Boston Society of Natural History*, 59:9–10 (April, 1931).

the romantic are extreme embodiments of tendencies found in harmonious equilibrium, though in varying proportions, it is true, in different men and different times, in the masters of any art and period. The classical mentality, we say, loves reason and order, values restraint, and deals with the formal and readily communicable norms of beauty. The romantic prefers nature, variety, the rich expression of an emotional world that is often deeply personal. But how satisfactory is this division even to professors of literature? What masterpiece is not to a large extent describable in both sets of terms—in terms of reason and nature and of restraint with vitality? The giants defy classification in such simple terms. Perhaps, after all, as good a modern definition as any of that protean word "humanism" is to use it to denote the mean between the classic and romantic extremes, between formal frigidity and emotional rapture, between reason and nature. At all events the term is so useful that I shall usurp it to explain why the greatest names of the history of science seem to me to fail miserably of inclusion in Ostwald's classification.

I am well aware that humanism is a dangerous term of many meanings. To begin, I shall not use it in its original sense, that of a man devoted to seeking out and restoring to general esteem the humane letters of antiquity, though it is in this limited sense that we apply the term to a host of Renaissance classical scholars from Petrach to Scaliger.

But out of this meaning of the word humanist there inevitably unfolds another which is often seized upon to express one aspect of the elusive and complex Renaissance spirit. The humanist was a man who, having studied the writings of antiquity, became imbued with the life-giving spirit which is so often found in them and turned to them for encouragement and inspiration in his struggle to give the Western world a fresh start and a new basis of sound learning. Humanism thus became identified with a protest against the decadent ecclesiasticism, the arid and disputatious learning—the wreck of the great medieval system of instruction—by which the humanists found themselves surrounded.

But this humanist spirit is by no means confined to the men of the Renaissance, though it flourished mightily in those great centuries. A feeling for the excitement and the promise of life; a sense of proportion; a dislike of cant, hypocrisy, and pedantry; a profound sense of life and a desire to partake of it totally—these are familiar aspects of the humanist spirit of the Renaissance. But something similar belongs in some degree to every age and is found in the best of human nature at all times. Modern scholarship has not failed to detect it in medieval man himself. The possession of this indefinable spirit is an indispensable condition for those great moments of intellectual achievement which we recognize as the noblest product of the human mind.

William James, in his famous lecture *On the One and the Many*, has, I think, pointed to the fundamental trait that sets apart the man whom we may identify, in whatever branch of human culture we find him, as the true humanist. He finds among philosophers tendencies which correspond to our loose but convenient categories of classic and romantic. Somewhat resembling the classic is the man obsessed with the Parmenidean quest for the *one*, the monistic urge to establish the unity of knowledge, at whatever cost to life and sanity. By contrast there is the pluralist, "your 'scholarly' mind, of encyclopedic, philological type," James calls him, "your man essentially of learning." Once again, these are extremes, and neither one satisfied the Jamesian need to explore the richness and the complexity of things. "What our intellect really aims at," he says, and he might well have specified his own, "is neither variety nor unity taken singly, but *totality* ... .Acquaintance with reality's diversities is as important as understanding their connexion."

Totality: now here is the word which seems to express the humanist aspiration. James gives us a somewhat apologetic simile which fits our scientific problem admirably:

> We are like fishes swimming in the sea of sense, bounded above by the superior element, but unable to breathe it pure or penetrate it. We get our oxygen from it, however; we touch it incessantly, now in this part, now in that, and every time we touch it we turn back into the water with our course redetermined and re-energized. The abstract ideas of which the air consists are indispensable to life, but irrespirable by themselves.[3]

How well this fits our scientists! Abstract investigations are necessary for re-energizing scientific life; but they cannot make up all of scientific experience; so science must dip back into the stream of life after each stratospheric ascension. There are men, we have seen, who by natural propensity spend an undue amount of time swimming in the aeriform fluid of abstraction and who not rarely float away wholly out of sight. There are the mathematical

[3] William James, *Pragmatism*, ed. Ralph Barton Perry (New York, 1943), p. 128.

philosophers of Laputa. But there are óthers who never leave the lower depths of the aquarium.

The greatest men of science seem to have possessed this Jamesian sense of totality. They have kept in close touch with nature, while deriving sustenance and direction from their speculative flights. What greater humanist in this very important sense can one possibly imagine than Galileo, the principal author of that idealized mechanical universe of which I have just spoken, and yet the most resourceful, gifted, and tireless of experimenters. Although he possessed a mind of great abstract power, he did more than any other man to extend the range of the human senses, since in the main the refracting telescope, the compound microscope, the pendulum clock, the thermometer, and the barometer can be traced to him. This sense of totality, this harmonious cultivation of both reason and nature, is a mark of the greatest scientific minds of all ages. We have it in Lavoisier, and we can find it also in Newton, in Helmholtz, and in Darwin, no less than in Galileo. Classics and romantics indeed!

Why, then, not call them humanists, since we find in them that rare concentration of power and balance of forces it has been our purpose to describe. If my analysis is even partially correct, this explains, and I think justifies, the inclusion among the classics of the world's literature certain, though perhaps not many, of the milestones of science. This practice at the University of Chicago and St. John's (which, by the way, was long ago advocated by Matthew Arnold) has called down upon Mr. Hutchins and Mr. Stringfellow Barr some severe criticism, and while I should not like to be called upon to defend the selection of, say, Ptolemy's *Almagest* or the *Conics* of Apollonius of Perga for the Great Books courses, the principle is sound. On what basis should we choose scientific books as representing a portion of the "best which has been thought and said in the world?" Only, it seems to me, when they show to a high degree this humanistic quality of dealing in some fashion with the world as a whole.

Let us now take Mr. James's advice and descend a bit from the level of abstraction to which he lured us, attempting to trace more prosily the influence of humanism upon the early growth of science.

Renaissance humanism, in both the broad and the restricted sense that I have used, had an intimate historical connection with the emergence of modern science in the period from the fifteenth to the eighteenth centuries. Concerning the influence upon science of the humanist movement, in our narrow definition, there can be little doubt. The scientific curiosity of Europe was immensely stimulated when scholarly scientists like Regiomontanus, Linacre, and Tartaglia and literary humanists with scientific interests like Giorgi and Commandino edited or translated the great classics of Hellenistic and Greco-Roman science which the Middle Ages had known imperfectly or not at all. An acquaintance with the original works of Ptolemy and Galen, of Vitruvius and Celsus, of Archimedes, Diophantus and Hero Alexandrinus spread abroad in well-edited and beautifully printed editions, lifted European science to a new level of technical accomplishment in astronomy, medicine, mathematics, and physics. The direct influence of this movement upon the work of Copernicus, Harvey, Galileo, and others is not difficult to discern.

But even humanism in the broader and more important

sense, so far from diverting attention from scientific interests as many scholars would have us believe, contributed, I think, to that more militant mood of scientific emancipation we associate with the generation of Gilbert, Galileo, and Francis Bacon. For it was from the earlier humanists that the scientific rebels borrowed the mordant phrases, already somewhat shopworn, with which they attacked the dim perspectives, the logic-chopping, the gigantic circularities of the scholastic mind. There is a Protestant spirit in science; and perhaps humanism paved the way for the scientific revolt in much the same way as it cleared the ground for Calvin and Luther and the religious Reformation.

The constant refrain of the early humanists had been for a restoration of honest learning. From the time of Vives, that extraordinary and little-known forerunner of Francis Bacon, a succession of able men tried to diagnose the causes of what they termed the "corruption of the arts" and concentrated their energies on the grandiose project of reforming all learning. In this program the reform of natural science was to play a prominent part. Vives in 1525 advocated a return to the original inquiring spirit of Aristotle, the adoption of the experimental method, and—to reform both medical training and the study of natural history—a return to nature and observation. The humanists were also by the same token pioneers in exposing the futility of the pseudo sciences. Pico wrote the classic refutation of astrology, while Vives, in treating of the corruption and decline of natural knowledge, emphasized how each pseudo science had contaminated its corresponding valid science.

Out of the early unsystematic criticism emerged the great

revolutionary nature philosophies of Telesio, Bruno, Campanella, and Francis Bacon, all hoping to construct a new philosophy upon a reformed science of nature. The humanist inspiration is quite evident, and it was the aim of all these systems to draw as fully as possible upon the new vistas which the expansion of Europe had revealed. Bacon, to cite the best-known example, expected his New Instauration to draw upon an exhaustive inventory of the resources of the world: experiments, observations, and histories without end; the reports of the travelers; the slowly accumulated secrets of the arts and crafts; and even the muddied waters of the pseudo sciences, which he rightly suspected of concealing useful truths.

Scientific progress was never wholly dependent upon these grandiose plans for a revival of learning, as detractors of Francis Bacon are always quick to point out. But it is an inescapable historical fact that by linking themselves consciously with this movement—whose leaders were not scientists, but philosophers and agitators tinged with the great secular movement of humanism—scientists less bold and original than Gilbert or Galileo were able to attain a sense of their collective identity, their common purpose, and the revolutionary significance of their activities for the modern world. It is for this reason that Francis Bacon became the household deity of the Royal Society of London and of the French Academy of Sciences. Under his banner the movement for a reform of philosophy through natural science became instead an antimetaphysical movement confined, as far as the new Academies were concerned, to the promotion of experimental science.

That the New Learning was antagonistic to the study of man, or even indifferent to it, would never have been admitted by any philosopher of the scientific way of life from Francis Bacon to Hume. But by the close of the seventeenth century the Baconian New Learning had already become fully equated, to a degree Bacon might not have relished, to the Experimental or Mechanical Philosophy, and one may well ask whether attention was not then so completely focused upon external nature that the ancient problems of man and of society were in danger of utter neglect. The enemies of the virtuosi were convinced that this was the case. In Shadwell's play, which I should like to quote once more, another disrespectful and exasperated niece describes her virtuoso uncle as "One, who has broken his Brains about the nature of Maggots, who has studied these twenty years to find out the several sorts of Spiders, and never cares for understanding mankind."

Have we more reliable evidence that this is a fair picture of the scientist's indifference to human problems? Is there anything to make us believe that the man of science of the late seventeenth century cared a fig for these weighty problems or felt that as scientists they were in any way responsible for their solution? Alas, the first evidence that comes to hand, the testimony of John Wallis and Robert Hooke as to the range of activity of the Royal Society, would seem to indicate not. "The business and design of the Royal Society," wrote Hooke, "is to improve the knowledge of natural things, and all useful Arts, Manufactures, Mechanik practices, Engynes and Inventions by Experiments—(not meddling with Divinity, Metaphysics, Moralls, Politicks, Grammar, Rhetorick, or Logick.)"[4]

---

[4] Quoted in Martha Ornstein, *The Role of Scientific Societies in the Seventeenth Century* (Chicago, 1928), pp. 108–109.

Yet in 1667 in his official defense of the Royal Society, the Reverend Thomas Sprat put matters more cautiously. After expounding the Baconian subdivision of all knowledge into the study of God, of Man, and of Nature, he did not hesitate to point out deferentially that the first was excluded from the work of the Society and that the study of external nature, as the proper field for the new fashion of experiment, claimed the principal allegiance of the investigators:

> In Men, may be consider'd the *Faculties*, the Operations of their *Souls*, the *Constitution of their Bodies* and the *Works of their Hands*. Of these, the *first* they omit; both because the Knowledge and Direction of them have been before undertaken by some *Arts* on which they have no mind to intrench, as the *Politicks*, *Morality* and *Oratory*; and also because the *Reason*, the *Understanding*, the *Tempers*, the *Will*, the *Passions* of Men, are so hard to be reduc'd to any certain Observation of the *Senses*, and afford so much room to the *Observers* to falsify or counterfeit, that if such Discourses should be once entertain'd, they would be in Danger of falling into *talking*, instead of *working*. . . .

Such subjects, he remarks, have therefore been kept out, but unlike Hooke, he suggests that this is only a temporary, tactical move. When the members of the society

> shall have made more Progress in *material* Things, they will be in a Condition of pronouncing more boldly on them [these subjects] too. For though

Man's *Soul* and *Body* are not only one natural
Engine (as some have thought) of whose Motions
of all Sorts, there may be as certain an Account
given, as if those of a Watch or Clock; yet by long
studying of the *Spirits*, of the *Blood*, of the
Nourishment, of the Parts, of the *Diseases*, of the
Advantages, of the Accidents which belong to
humane Bodies (all which will come within their
Province) there may, without Question, be very
near Guesses made, even at the more *exalted* and
immediate Actions of the Soul. . . .[5]

In this paper I have been arguing that the scientist and
the humanist have more in common than is usually supposed. I have tried to show how humanism affected the
growth of science, and have even suggested that Renaissance humanism may have contributed to the great scientific rebellion of the Age of Galileo. It remains now to ask
if the scientific movement did exert an appreciable influence upon the study of man and human society, and
whether within a reasonable time someone attempted to
fulfill Sprat's prophecy that physiological studies might
contribute to a better understanding of man's nature.

The first serious attempt to make a scientific study of
human society is due to a man intimately associated with
the scientific and historical currents of his time, and it is
based on a theory of human nature which the discussions
of the humanists and the rise of modern science—in particular the famous Quarrel of the Ancients and Moderns—

[5] Thomas Sprat, *The History of the Royal Society of London, For
the Improving of Natural Knowledge*. The Third Edition Corrected
(London, 1722), pp. 82–83.

had brought to the fore: the theory of the essential in-
variance of human nature through time and space, and the
belief—which Fontenelle put into the mouth of Socrates
in his *Dialogues des Morts*—that man was a part of the
"general order of nature."

Montesquieu's *Esprit des Lois*, published just two hundred years ago, is, I believe, the first book of any consequence on political and social questions to be influenced to
any degree by the scientific movement. Although Machia-
velli's *The Prince* has been loosely referred to as a "scientific" manual of practical politics, and Thomas Hobbes
hoped *The Leviathan* would make him the Copernicus or
the Harvey of moral philosophy, Montesquieu's *Spirit of
the Laws* is yet the first book to be genuinely saturated by
the spirit, the example, the point of view, the method, and
even the findings of natural science. Auguste Comte, for
better or for worse the accredited father of sociology,
has pointed out that Montesquieu was one of the first
to approach the whole study of human institutions from
the point of view of modern science and to develop the
idea that men were as subject to invariable laws as the rest
of animate and inanimate nature.

The *Esprit des Lois* opens with Montesquieu's classic
definition of Law as expressing in the broadest sense "the
necessary relations that arise from the nature of things."
God created and conserves the world and all its creatures,
including man himself, according to fixed laws which resemble, and in fact include, the mathematical uniformities
discovered by the scientist. Man in society is subject to
these laws too, and man-made legal systems have unconsciously reflected them. Montesquieu's development of
his theory is designed to escape the deterministic conse-

quences which the broadly phrased statement of it would seem to imply. The words "natural law" in reality embrace two sorts of things. First there are the rigid, inflexible, inescapable *physical* laws of the universe which govern man as part of material nature. Then there are the natural *moral* laws which exist, as it were, potentially, and govern man as a rational creature through his right reason. They are normative principles detectable in the rules of justice and equity. These laws are invariable like those of the scientist, but since man is a spontaneous being subject to error they are not invariably obeyed as the scientific laws must be.

It is, of course, the main purpose of the *Esprit des Lois* to study the systems of positive law that the peoples of the world have set up for themselves. Montesquieu is not concerned, like Grotius or Puffendorff or Vattel, to expound the normative principles and say what should be the practices common to all men. He is concerned with the deviations from these norms observable in different parts of the world and in different ages. What causes these differences? If human nature and human reason depend only upon the moral natural law and human reason, the positive laws should be everywhere the same. But in every nation the systems of positive law are applied by fallible human beings living under somewhat different conditions. The variations and particularities are introduced by the action upon man of the physical environment and the deterministic laws of the physical world. The legal systems and institutions of the world thus result from the simultaneous operation of the two sets of natural laws.

The problem is posed as a problem in biology might be, and is tackled by a method similar to the comparative method which a biologist might use in studying the homologous structures of related animal groups in order to discover the special environmental adaptation in each case. Montesquieu is interested in the great patterns detectable in human society, but he also wishes to describe the variations and particularities. He sets up a whole program for the comparative sociological study of the peoples of the world far beyond the capacities of a single man, even of his great genius and diligence, to carry out. Human laws should be interpreted:

> relative to the physical characteristics of the country, and to whether its climate is frigid, torrid or temperate, to the quality of its soil, to its location, to its size, to the mode of life of its people (whether laborers, hunters, or shepherds). They should be considered in terms of the amount of liberty the constitution can allow; to the religion of the inhabitants, their inclinations, wealth, commerce, customs and manner.[6]

In the *Esprit des Lois* Montesquieu takes up these problems one after the other. Several famous and much criticized sections deal with the influence of climate. It is here that he undertakes the sort of application of current physiological ideas which Sprat had adumbrated, and by the same token commits the ordinary error of many who have tried to borrow from science; namely, that of taking as literally and permanently true the scientific theories and hypotheses of one's own time; whereas about the only thing that the social sciences can safely take from the biological sciences is the knowledge that the biological sciences

[6] *Esprit des Lois*, Book I, Chap. 3.

are already much more complicated than the physical sciences and their theories correspondingly more tentative.

To understand the influences that led Montesquieu to adopt the now long-extinct fiber theory of the iatrophysicists requires a word about his scientific background.[7] His education, at the hands of the Oratorians of Juilly, was mainly classical, but early in his brief legal career he devoted himself passionately to the study of science. Though seemingly ignorant, in the main, of Newtonian science, he was an avowed Cartesian both in physics and biology. He was a life-long member and supporter of the Academy of Bordeaux, before which as a young man he read a number of scientific papers: on the cause of the echo, on the possible function of the mysterious suprarenal glands, and on the "gravity of bodies." He projected a great Natural History of the Earth to be based on physical, *i.e.*, presumably Cartesian, principles. His published correspondence reveals a wide scientific acquaintance and his *Pensées*—voluminous notebooks of jottings on all subjects, unpublished until 1899—show an incredibly diverse scientific curiosity.[8] He has notes on the absorption of the thymus; on the coronary and fetal circulations; on the significance of fossils; on soil exhaustion; on the mechanics of bird flight; on the teeth of mammals and the correlation of their morphology with animals' feeding habits. He seems even to have had a

[7] The scientific interests of Montesquieu are mentioned by his principal biographers but have never been given adequate treatment, especially in view of the materials made available by the publication of the papers from La Brede and the *Correspondance* brought out by Gebeliu and Morize in 1914. The material of this paper is preliminary to a more detailed study of the scientific influences upon Montesquieu.

[8] *Pensées et Fragments inédits de Montesquieu.* (Published by Baron Gaston de Montesquieu, 2 volumes; Bordeaux, 1899.)

clearly formulated theory of the "multiplication" of species, that is, of the evolution of the present multiplicity of forms from a few ancestral types. He even believed that the extinction of species was somehow involved in the process, a view that would have shocked Cuvier. He was interested in microscopy and in such medical problems as inoculation for smallpox, theories of contagion, the course of epidemics, and above all the relation of climate to disease.

That climate could determine the traits and institutions of mankind was a very old theory. It had been advanced in antiquity in the Hippocratic treatise, *Airs, Waters and Places*, in which there was a revived interest shortly before Montesquieu's time.[9] It had been used by Jean Bodin in the sixteenth century, and more recently had been advanced by people as different as the traveler Chardin, the Abbé du Bos, and the scientific publicist Fontenelle. But Montesquieu offers in addition a physiological theory— a mechanical, iatrophysical theory—to explain just how climate can bring about changes in the human constitution and hence account for the inclinations, laws, customs, and manners of different peoples. This explanation is based on the presumed action of air upon the fibers of which the body was believed to be built. The fibers of the body respond to the temperature, humidity, and impurities of the air—cold, dry air shortening and compressing the fibers, moist, warm air having the opposite effect. The motor re-

---

[9] Thomas Sydenham (1624–1689) and Hermann Boerhaave (1668–1738) were leaders in this Hippocratic revival. This is reflected in the space given by Daniel Leclerc to Hippocrates in his *History of Medicine* (1699). In 1734 Francis Clifton brought out an English translation of *Airs, Waters and Places*.

sponse of voluntary muscles, the pumping action of the heart, the efficiency of venous return are all influenced by the tone of the fibers. Because of this, people in cold climates are men of action, courage, and creativeness, lovers of liberty and national independence, given to military prowess but also enjoying a high incidence of suicide. The people of warm climates are correspondingly slothful and conservative; among them the institutions of slavery and monasticism flourish, and they tend to produce philosophic and religious systems which favor contemplation and inaction. A similar action of the air is invoked to account for the difference in temperament of peoples. Sensory nerve trunks are composed of bundles of nerves which Montesquieu believed to be spread out, like the frayed end of a thread, at the skin or sensory organ. Heat expands the epidermal area and splays out the nerve endings, producing finer sensitivity and discrimination. Cold, on the contrary, brings them together as the epidermal layer contracts; this tends to deaden sensation. It is clearly evident that denizens of hot climates must be more sensual and greater voluptuaries than persons condemned to live in cold climates. It is in this connection that Montesquieu cites in the *Esprit des Lois* his own microscopic observations of a sheep's tongue, where he saw the organs of taste seem to disappear and shrink together under the action of cold.[10]

A French scholar, Abbé Joseph Dedieu, long ago identified the principal source from which Montesquieu drew his fiber theory of the influence of climate.[11] This is a little

[10] *Esprit des Lois*, Book XIV, Chap. 2.

[11] Joseph Dedieu, *Montesquieu et la tradition politique anglaise en France—les sources anglaises de "L'Esprit des Lois"* (Paris, 1909). See especially Chapter VII, "Les rapports des lois avec le climat."

book by John Arbuthnot—physician and member of the
Royal Society of London, wit and satirist, close friend of
Gay and Swift, and inventor of the British national symbol, John Bull—entitled *An Essay Concerning the Effects
of Air on Human Bodies*. It was first published in 1733 and
became available in a French translation in 1742.

It is a rare and interesting little octavo.[12] In showing how
the air can exert its effect on the fibers and fluids of the
body, Dr. Arbuthnot gives a masterful abridgment of all
that had been discovered about the properties of air to his
own time. The ideas are based upon the discoveries of Robert Boyle, Robert Hooke, Francis Hauksbee, Stephen Hales,
and Edmund Halley—all members of the English school
that had centered its attention on the study of air—and upon
the great chemical textbook of the Dutch physician Hermann Boerhaave, the first work dealing mainly with what today we would call physical chemistry. Through this little
book an extraordinary amount of recent scientific information was thereby made compactly available to Montesquieu. Arbuthnot, moreover, combined the anatomist's fiber
theory with a physico-chemical theory of the action of air
upon these fibers and performed experiments to confirm
his theory. "I have found," he wrote, "that the single
fibers, both of vegetables and animals, are lengthened by
water or by moist air; a fiddle string moisten'd with water
will sink a note in a little time."

Arbuthnot presents in a nutshell, and if possible more
bluntly than Montesquieu, the fiber theory of the action

---

[12] John Arbuthnot, *An Essay Concerning the Effects of Air on Human
Bodies* (1733; French translation, 1742).

of climate, even going so far as to discuss its effects on human societies:

> Governments [Arbuthnot wrote] stamp the Manners, but cannot change the Genius and Temper of the Inhabitants; and as far as they are unrestrained by Laws, their Passions, and consequently their National Virtues and Vices will bear some Conformity with the Temperature of the Air.[13]

At one point Arbuthnot illustrates his argument with an example Montesquieu may not have appreciated. He attributes the characteristic frivolity of the French to the persistence of climatic factors. He cites the Emperor Julian as saying that Lutetia had "more Comedians, Dancers and Fidlers than there were Citizens," a picture he felt to be still valid for the eighteenth century, "and I believe," he continued, "if a Race of Laplanders were transplanted thither, in a few Years they would be found in the condition describ'd by the Emperor Julian."[14]

Perhaps you remember that Voltaire disposed of Montesquieu's idea that courage and military prowess depend only upon temperature by pointing out that Laps and Samoiedes were not remarkable for their courage, while in eighty years the Arabs of Mohammed conquered a territory larger than the whole Roman Empire. I wonder what he would have said about Arbuthnot's climate theory of language:

> I will venture to add another Observation, which, tho' it may seem a little to much refin'd

---

[13] *Ibid.*, p. 150.
[14] *Ibid.*, pp. 149–150.

[we would say far-fetched], is not improbable: That the Air has an Influence in forming the Languages of Mankind: The serrated close way of Speaking of Northern Nations, may be owing to their Reluctance to open their Mouth wide in cold Air, which must make their Language abound in Consonants; whereas from a contrary Cause, the Inhabitants of warmer Climates opening their Mouths, must form a softer Language, abounding in Vowels.

Another Observation is, that People in windy Countries naturally speak loud, to make themselves be heard in the open Air.[15]

I have perhaps dwelt too long upon Arbuthnot's theory and the use that Montesquieu made of it, but I would not want to leave you with the feeling that it is the best that Montesquieu took from the scientific influences that surrounded him and that helped shape his intellect, for I believe it rather to have been the worst. "All the sciences are good," Montesquieu wrote in a sentence that reveals much, "and mutually assist one another."[16] A great motto, it is true, if one is suitably wary of his borrowings.

Let me then conclude on the note with which I began this discussion of Montesquieu. It was his determination to study man as a part of physical as well as moral nature, to view him as responding to invariable physical laws, that constitutes Montesquieu's great achievement. He asserted the axioms and laid down the principles that should lead to a science, or more accurately a natural history, of man.

15 *Ibid.*, pp. 153–154.
16 Montesquieu, *Pensées*, I:460.

He made a bold and historic attempt to show by writing a sociology of law how this sort of thing should be done. We must forgive him his climates and his fiber theory. He borrowed them as freely, and trusted them as guilelessly, as many modern scholars borrow and trust the equally tentative guesses of modern psychology. It is the spirit and method of Montesquieu, I feel, by which we should judge him.

But what of his method? There are those who believe with Albert Sorel that Montesquieu is mainly a *génie généralisateur*, more Euclidean and Cartesian than scientific in any modern sense, that his book—despite the significant lack of classic order in its composition—is a good example of the dogmatic, a priori reasoning of a sheltered scholar, a typical product of the mathematical rationalism of the Age of Reason. This I feel confuses the method of exposition with the method of discovery. The *Esprit des Lois* must be read in the light of the *Pensées*, which are the chips and shavings from Montesquieu's workshop. Here he appears more Baconian than Cartesian, professes his distaste for the mathematical mind, proclaims himself as "not fond of opinions" and an enemy of rationalist systems. But did he have an insight into the so-called inductive aspects of natural science? I believe he did. The *Esprit des Lois* itself was not spun simply out of his inner consciousness, though there is a deceptive sentence in the book which has led some persons to think this was the case. Reference to his classic blunder about the British Constitution can blind us to the enormous reading, the extensive travel, the tireless energy, the active correspondence which went into the *Esprit des Lois*.

But as proof of his grasp of the scientific approach to

difficult problems let me borrow from the *Pensées* his
contribution to a burning medical question of the day,
the study of the epidemiology of the plague. This is what
he says:

> It seems to me that in Europe we are not in a
> position to make proper observations on the
> plague. This disease which is transplanted here
> does not display its natural characteristics. It
> varies a great deal with the differences in climate,
> without taking into account the fact that since it
> is not always present, and there being intervals
> of whole centuries between its appearances, we
> cannot make continual observations. Moreover,
> the observers are so distraught with fear that
> they are not able to make any at all.
>
> But accurate, enlightened and well-paid ob-
> servers should be sent into the regions where this
> disease is epidemic and appears every year, as in
> Egypt and several places in Asia.
>
> We ascertain what are the causes of it, what
> seasons are favorable or unfavorable, and observe
> the winds, the rains, the nature of the climate;
> what ages and temperaments are the most vul-
> nerable; what remedies, preventives and varia-
> tions of the disease there are. We should have
> observations from many different times and
> places, and use any information that certain
> countries might be able to give us. [17]

This proposal—with its echoes of Hippocrates—can only
command the respect of anyone of scientific training and

[17] *Ibid.,* I:487–488.

experience. How can the same man have written in the
Esprit des Lois: "When I discovered my principles, everything came to me . . . I laid down the principles and I saw
the special cases fit in by themselves." Was Montesquieu
a man of the classic type, or did the Baconian "romantic"
disposition predominate. Who can tell? But perhaps the
answer to the enigma is that like Galileo, the founder of
modern physics, Montesquieu, the father of the social
sciences, had something of the spirit William James attempted to describe, a spirit too big and complex to be
readily pigeonholed, with a love for both abstract con-
structions and the tangled wilderness of the real world:
in a word, a scientific humanist.

10 The Humanities as a Basis for a Community of Peoples

Howard Lee Nostrand

THE symposium committee has consented to let me present for discussion a subject that is not always discussed with much profit: the question of what the humanities have to offer to international relations. The committee suggested a title bolder than I had proposed; yet on contemplating the idea of "the humanities as a *basis* for a community of peoples," I found it not nearly so presumptuous as I first thought, and willingly adopted the proposition as the topic for our inquiry.

I propose that we entirely avoid extolling the wisdom of the humanities and lamenting how all that wisdom goes unheeded in practical affairs. Suppose we begin this time from the other end and try first of all to define what is needed for the conduct of international relations that might come from the direction of the humanities. As far as we can, let us look at the need as it appears to people engaged in the operations of world affairs. To interpret their conception of the need, we shall want next to stop long enough to collect our own previous thoughts on the subject. Then we should be able, with a fresh perspective, to inquire what we in the humanities need most to contribute to that great cause of our time, the creation of a world community out of the present world divided and armed against itself.

Since the end purpose of our inquiry is a partial definition of the humanities we may be allowed to define the

term only in a very general way at the start. May we
assume that the humanities center around human values,
in contrast on the one side with the overlapping province
of religion, which centers around spiritual values, and on
the other side with the natural and social sciences, which,
as sciences, can deal with values only as facts. Hence if
we find something that needs to be done about human
values more than to study existing situations, we shall
consider that we have a problem for those who devote
themselves to the humanities. We must hasten to recognize, too, that the manners of cultivating the humanities
are very diverse; so diverse that there can be no thought
of regimenting all scholars or artists into any activity,
however desirable it might appear.

I

A recent assignment gave me the occasion to talk with
a large number of United States officials concerned with
foreign relations. The American Council on Education,
in connection with a project to help colleges and universities re-examine together their changing role in world affairs, had asked me to study the actual state of and further
possibilities of cooperation between these educational institutions and the government agencies which are working
in the same sectors of cultural relations. I consequently
found myself talking or corresponding with some officials
at policy-making levels where I had never before thought
of intruding. I felt a bit out of place, all too aware that
humanities professors have not been accustomed to frequent this administrative world. Yet in one interview after
another I discovered a mind concerned over some issue of
those broad human purposes, beyond the level of the tech-

nical and instrumental, which I recognized as the real subject of my own teaching of literature.

One administrator I talked with is convinced that the Economic Recovery Program, before it can achieve any self-perpetuating reconstruction, must somehow rise above the objective of material prosperity alone to restore the fundamental faith that striving is worth the trouble. This, to be sure, is a spiritual matter, at least for many people. Yet if the faith is to take the peculiar form of striving to build a good society, it cannot do without an accompanying conviction that it is possible to make common cause with human beings of diverse nationalities and creeds. To provide a rational basis for that conviction, and to persuade people to give thought to it, is decidedly a problem at the level of the humanities.

A number of policy makers criticized the fourth point of President Truman's inaugural address for not going beyond projects of technological services and capital investment abroad to help other peoples develop proficiency and leadership in the less tangible achievements of a culture which are just as essential for social stability, self-respect, and wisdom in world affairs. Yet no one felt he quite had the answer to the question of how the President could have included this among his objectives without incurring criticism at home for a vague program of doubtful efficiency and criticism abroad for imposing the aims of the United States rather than implementing the aspirations of the local culture. To answer this practical question calls for study of what purposes are common to both cultures and what pattern of local initiative and United States aid would most efficiently advance their realization.

One able thinker I called on was much concerned over a

certain lack in the training of public servants. In peace as well as in war, she observes, we are strong at the technical level; we excel at carrying out details of any plan; but we suffer from a scarcity of minds that can select and strike a wise balance among the larger purposes that approach government's ultimate reason for being.

As I look back I am surprised not to have encountered the criticism common among unofficial Americans that we have prosecuted the cold war too much on the level of outsmarting the Russian government and too little on the level of defining great human purposes for which our rights and freedoms are means and setting the example of living up to them at the sacrifice of special privileges and discriminatory advantages. The general concern I did discover again and again, however, certainly centered around the need of which this is a special case: the need for a more vivid and uninterrupted consciousness of humane values in the conduct of international affairs.

It was not surprising to find this concern among the officers in charge of cultural relations. From a quite different office, however, one influencing the providing of funds for cultural relations, came the clearest views on the danger that the long-range, two-way development of cooperation in research, education, social welfare, and the other "cultural" fields can be turned into a hypocrisy by just one officer who judges their usefulness according to whether they give him an immediate negotiating advantage over the representatives of a rival country. Here we have a recognized need, partly for a more philosophical education of officers and partly for a better public understanding and support of "cultural" programs as a new instrument of international relations; but either side brings

us back to the same fundamental need we have already
approached from several directions.

Before we summarize these opinions on needs of United
States foreign relations, let us add one policy maker's
thinking on the need for an intergovernmental agency.
He was concerned, as an interested outsider, that the
United Nations Educational, Scientific and Cultural Organization appeared to be devoting its energy to the projects of special-interest groups and was missing its central
mission, which should have to do with formulating basic
common purposes of cultural relations. I cannot agree
with him that Unesco's heterogeneous program items constitute an undue dispersion of effort. Most of them seem
to me useful services to groups whose end effect is unselfish,
and as for the remainder of the items, considerable ex-
perimentation seems only prudent in so new a venture.
But this was an accessory point. I do agree with him that
Unesco's central mission should have to do with finding
an international common ground of human purposes. In
fact I consider that a start has been made in the right
direction, which I shall bring up later as one constructive
proposal.

Can we sum up briefly the need that preoccupies these
various public servants? It seems to me to resolve down
to a few recurrent elements. It is a need on the part of the
officials themselves, the private specialists to whom they
look for advice, and the electorate as a whole to be able
to visualize more clearly, to apply more efficiently and
steadfastly, and to express more cogently certain human
purposes or values for which technology and prosperity,
even human rights and freedoms, are instrumental, particularly those values which can be pursued cooperatively

by peoples of different national loyalties and different beliefs as to the ultimate explanation and sanction of human life.

Certainly if values are the center of gravity of the humanities, it should be possible for scholars in the humanities to do something more effective than has been done about this need without departing from their own proper concerns. And the fact that the need is appreciated by people charged with the day-to-day conduct of foreign relations provides the kind of opportunity which we ought not to pass over. I have the impression that the opportunity has vastly improved in recent months, though in this I may be wrong, since I had never before had occasion to make such a sampling of policy-making officials. I am certain, however, that the concern I discovered was no ephemeral result of a moment's wondering what use might be found for academic minds. The opinions evidenced considerable previous thought, and the most advanced of them had been written down on some earlier occasion. I am equally certain that an important movement is in progress among the agencies dealing with cultural relations to tighten their provision for their respective responsibilities, and this process is leading inevitably to a re-examination of underlying purposes.

II

What background do we bring from our various provinces of the humanities to interpret the need as it is felt by those engaged in the practical operations? The very diversity of the answers that would come out of this group, if we had time for a full discussion of that question, leads me to emphasize for my part the profound difficulty of bringing about any higher proficiency in the visualization and in the application and cogent expression of broad human purposes.

Most of the administrators I talked with I think underestimated this difficulty. Some of them spoke of "thinking through" the problems before them, as though one could count on finding ground under his feet at every step from the immediate situation to a satisfying end objective, and could count also on finding other men of good will following the same path to the same conclusion.

The fact is more nearly that our contemporary knowledge, as it bears on the conduct of life, is a maze of curves extrapolated from small fields of proved validity into the field of ethics, where they contradict one another. The individual can ignore the fields whose implications he dislikes, and so make an insecure peace with himself, but at the expense of any dependable basis for harmony of purpose with others who have made a different arbitrary selection.

Even among specialists in one branch of the humanities, such as painting, how often it happens that one chooses to live with masterpieces of the past, which imply that we live in an understandable world, while his colleague prefers to contemplate in the art of his contemporaries a disquieting, unsettled world which he is not sure anyone ever can understand. The one has no use for the old world which people thought they understood, while the other finds all the straining of modern art uncalled for. They feud on; and the administrator who seeks out the advice of the expert, whichever one he finds, goes away with a decidedly arbitrary notion of the sector of the humanities he has visited.

Cultural diversity is a good thing: an enrichment of individual life. But the diversity of contradictory general implications, such as mechanism generalized from the physical sciences, evolutionism from the biological, and so on, leads to confusion and cross purposes rather than to enrichment. And no sound reconciliation can be brought about until the field of validity of each implication for human life is carefully defined.

Not only have the great cultures of our time grown more heterogeneous in their directive ideas than the nonspecialist would imagine, but several other factors increase the difficulty of individual conviction and of agreement on questions of values.

In the mentality of great numbers of people, the bottom has dropped out of certain great ideals such as brotherly love, the spirit of reverence, and that philosophical tranquillity which our Latin American neighbors still speak of, much more frequently than we, as *serenidad*. Consider the ideal of brotherly love, to which we appeal in our efforts to improve the relations among peoples and among the so-called races. Some contemporaries are able to make brotherly love their sincere intention because it is a divine command. A few others have built a steadfast conviction upon the postulate that the realization of human value should be maximized, reasoning their way from that beginning to the propositions that altruism is a better intention than selfishness and brotherly love a better spirit than hatred or indifference. This diversity of approach is no detriment to cooperation. But a vast majority have no real conviction on any basis, and for them brotherly love proves to be a shallow sentimentality, essentially egotistical, powerless to combat old habits of discrimination at home, and disgusting, in its patronizing solicitude, to the newly met foreigners on whom it is lavished.

Beyond the difficulties of confusion and shallowness lie still others which we create by our inexpertness in dealing with human values. The familiar truism that technology has outstripped the ability to make it serve mankind has endless consequences which are far from commonplace observations. One is the drab and unpoetic symbols with which we try so ineffectively to keep large objectives before our minds. Another is the fact that when we do turn in this direction we are inclined to expect too much, as though a rational Q.E.D. could resolve away historic emotional antagonisms and the competition for scarce material goods.

To the same inexpertness we may attribute the fault of conceiving values in terms of things we know better. For example a prominent man and real thinker said recently, referring to the need of carrying United States assistance beyond the material level, that "we must export freedom." Such infelicity of expression is a minor form of the fault, even when it leads to a misestimation of us by people of other cultures. After all, we do mean to export freedom, at promotional rates or even gratis, with our compliments. But the fault goes deeper when we find ourselves unwittingly thinking and feeling the meanings peculiar to the humanities in the terms of imagined analogies or contrasts with the materials of the sciences. The process of research within a small frame of reference, unwanted variables being regarded for the purpose as constant or as irrelevant, does not lead to the sort of experience and judgment most needed in the humanities. It is by false analogy to the sciences that we attack problems of the humanities in this narrow way; they require a mind of breadth, alert to discover the import of all sorts of knowledge for the conduct of human life. On the other hand, we draw a false contrast if we regard the humanities as inscrutably esoteric and unaccountable to reason. Those who maintain that the scientific method suddenly stops somewhere in the biological or the social sciences neglect the extremely important continuity of the same reasonable approach, which requires always what rigor is permitted by the materials at hand and is necessary for useful conclusions, from the sciences to history, ethics, esthetics and religion—extremely important, I insist, because this reasonable approach is the only possible basis of agreement among individuals and among cultures upon knowledge about human values just as well as upon knowledge about the physical cosmos or human nature.

Inexpert as we are in handling the confused values of our own culture, we find ourselves now caught up in the swift currents of an increasing exchange between cultures. It would not be enough to know our own mind, even if we could. We must somehow learn at the same time to understand and accept with good grace the role of a minority culture in a world community.

It is for all these reasons that it seems to me naïve to speak of "thinking through" the practical decisions that involve human values, unless one has in mind a tremendous cooperative enterprise of administrators, specialists in the various branches of the humanities, and specialists in the sciences that study values as matters of fact to overcome the difficulties we have reviewed. If we could put with this sketchy account the previous thinking which you would be able to contribute, it seems reasonable to suppose that more difficulties would have to be added to the list, and few if any could be resolved to our collective satisfaction.

One of the executives I talked with, the one who feared the subservience of cultural programs to short-range advantages of political negotiation, had evidently reflected upon the need for such a cooperative venture, for he remarked that if the colleges and universities were clear in their thinking and united on some points of possible common agreement, they would be able with proper channels of communication to exert considerable influence on policy and in fact would meet with a rapid response. This view is certainly in line with the general philosophy of democratic government as representing the will of the people, and it illustrates the specific principle of our government officials in the matter of cultural relations, that they build their policy and their services around private leadership to the full extent that private individuals and organizations can be persuaded to take the initiative.

But if we envisage this sort of partnership between administrators and scholars, we must reckon with another difficulty besides those we have already cited. History has not allowed us to forget the conclusion which Socrates reached in the Fifth Book of the *Republic*, that until either the philosophers become kings or kings take seriously to philosophizing, until political power and philosophy converge, there is no end of bad times in sight for the city states, or for the human race either. Since Plato's time those who govern may have made some progress; we certainly have

found a number of them in this inquiry who have taken
seriously to philosophizing. To judge whether the philosophers have made corresponding progress toward the mer-
ger, it would be interesting to find out whether the conspicuous examples like Lord Balfour, Lord Keynes, Jan
Smuts, and Benedetto Croce are supported by an advance
among the many less famous workers in the humanities.
But perhaps the most conspicuous development since fifth-
century Athens is the division and subdivision of both
kings and philosophers into specialized types until it is a
physical impossibility for either one simply to turn to the
other.

III

Exploit as we may the comic element in our plight, one
encouraging thought at least remains to serve as the start-
ing point for constructive effort. When we face the danger
of war, government for all its complexity is still able to
turn to the natural scientists and find a basis for technological superiority. In the great depression of the thirties, the more difficult feat was performed of turning to the
social scientists to provide the basis for a remedial economic and social program. This was more difficult for
several reasons which interest us because the humanities
have the same disadvantages in more acute form. The
reasons seem to have been that the goal was less definite
than the goal of "victory," the motive was less compelling
than the motive of self-preservation, our mastery in the
social sciences is less sure than in the natural sciences, and
while the great destruction planned in warfare is presumed
to be at the expense of other peoples, the destruction of

special privilege that lurks in the best-intentioned social reforms is bound to alienate influential citizens at home.

Now we find ourselves in a continuing international crisis. This country is engaging in material and technical reconstruction over a good part of the planet. Yet thoughtful administrators see that this effort will not suffice unless it is accompanied by clearer conception, steadier application, and more convincing expression of the common purposes that constitute the vital ideas of a world community. To find a basis for a constructive program in this area, it is logical that the responsible administrators should turn to those who devote their lives to the humanities—provided they can find us. But what can we do?

We can, first of all, offer ourselves as we are for the temporary assignments or careers that require our individual competences; and this is very important.

Cultural attachés and visiting professors and members of field parties capable of interpreting the best in their own culture can have a profound effect on mutual confidence and the common understanding of purposes between peoples. Humanists qualified to take such positions for a couple of years' leave of absence have been so scarce that executives who fully appreciate the usefulness of such interchange between public and private life have been unable to carry it out. More of us should make a hobby of some language and area in order to be prepared for service of this sort.

Humanists are in demand likewise for briefer assignments as consultants in their branches of research and education on invitations which come more and more frequently to the United States. A mission in the social sciences and the humanities, headed by Professor Charles E. Martin of the University of Washington, recently spent a valuable three months in Japan at the request of the Military Government, a request initiated by Japanese scholars anxious to overcome the effects of isolationism and also aware that their contacts with the West must range beyond the fields covered by a second scientific mission which was in Japan at the same time on American initiative.

The humanities also need international organization and planning among the groups of specialized scholars and teachers. In fact, relatively little of the available resources has gone to the humanities, not because the work to be done was less vital than that of the sciences but for lack of comparable organization and planned programs. International professional organizations require hours of often thankless devotion and may be recommended as a specific to any humanist who seeks to do penance for having neglected his world responsibilities.

Then there are the countless services one can give on a college campus to advance international cultural relations through the interchange of students and teachers, provision for those from abroad to take an intimate part in campus and community life, better general education and professional training as they bear on international understanding, and so on. The greatest need of this sort, in my estimation, is for a planning agency among the faculty and students to go far beyond the publicizing of fellowship opportunities, far beyond even the badly needed establishment of lines of communication with all the relevant agencies, to assure that the institution with the help of its community is taking initiative throughout the range of its obligations to the ideal, or the necessity, of world community.

All these things have their importance. But our inquiry leads to deeper implications for the humanities which we must not allow ourselves to forget as we busy ourselves running hither and yon to meetings.

I would urge, though this may meet with hearty disagreement, that many of us are needed to concentrate on three fundamental activities that seem decidedly scarce in the lives of those who represent the humanities in the twentieth century. The first has to do with knowledge about values, the second, experience of values, and the third, artistic expression such as to convert abstract conclusions into social forces.

Knowledge about values, in order to accomplish the purposes and overcome the difficulties we have considered, calls for nothing less than a synthesis of each modern culture built around its ideas vital for human conduct: ideas of method or valid roads to truth; factual concepts that guide the conduct of life; and ideas of human purpose, or values, in accord with the supposed nature of the world, to which must be added descriptive knowledge of the extent to which the values are now put into practice and of the means by which they can be further realized. The dangers of thus formulating a living culture are hard to avoid, but not impossible. The synthesis does not need to be either vague and sentimental or dogmatic and dictatorial; nor need it represent the moot points as anything but precisely what they are. An enterprise of this sort requires collaboration from all fields of learning, yet the

burden of organizing the venture falls within the humanities. Once the ever tentative and evolving syntheses of
the various cultures are in a state to be compared together,
it will be possible to see their common ground and no
doubt to extend it as common world conditions press all
the extant cultures into some measure of convergent evolution.

It is the formulation of this common ground that might
well become a cohesive center for Unesco's far-flung program. The step in the right direction which I mentioned
earlier, in partial answer to a criticism of Unesco, is item
5.51 of the program for 1949: "To carry out a comparative study of cultures concerning the ideas held by one
country, or by a group within a country, of their own cultures and the relations of those cultures with others. . . ."
This may seem at first a foolhardy undertaking. Yet the
necessity for it seems inescapable, and the work of thinkers
like F. S, C, Northrop and Oliver Reiser, the currents of
thought brought together by organizations such as the
Foundation for Integrated Education, and the experience
of an interdepartmental "synthesis seminar" which began
in 1941 at the University of Washington and out of which
has grown the Unesco program item just quoted all go to
show that the idea of synthesizing a contemporary culture
around its vital ideas is no mirage of all the known and
the unknown, as some of us feared it might be.

But the knowledge about values is nothing more than
allusive and indeed misleading verbiage unless it is kept
in the most intimate contact with experience of those
values. We tend to regard such experience as too common
a thing to be worth collecting; yet unless we constantly

take notice and reflect how fresh experience embarrasses our past generalizations, we fall short of the essential quality of a life devoted to the humanities. It is no luxury but a necessity in such a life to stop and enjoy the beauty of a painting, of a deed well done, or of a spring evening. In this attentiveness to experience of human value we have grown mediocre amidst the noise and bustle of the twentieth century. One may be a good scientist without taking the slightest interest in people, but one cannot be a good student of humanity without indulging an insatiable curiosity to understand the personalities that come into his life.

A teacher of the humanities, therefore, can afford to serve the relations between peoples in a number of ways that are now neglected without feeling that he is robbing his professional development. He can spend the hours it takes to know intimately a visitor from a distant culture. He can afford the long succession of talks, month in and month out, to lead his own advisees out of the confines of a provincial mind to his own world horizon. And he can give years of sympathetic study to the literature and art which are the autobiography of a people in order to be able to teach his young compatriots something that escapes all the sciences, in so far as they are sciences: the experience of how it feels to live in a countryside, a tradition, and a language markedly different from one's own.

The third and last problem on which I urge that we concentrate would make us add something to the scheme of a cultural synthesis which we blocked out a moment ago. For it means that we should ask not only "What are the vital ideas of our time," but "What great symbols does each possess, and how can those ideas that are as yet mere abstractions be endowed with something of human life, among them the concepts of world community and world government?"

We need more genius in the creation of symbols and a fresh view of the possibilities of symbolism. Our greatest difficulty here is the lack of well-formulated ideas, responsible to the best knowledge of the time; and this we have already discussed under the head of knowledge about values. Yet this lack is not the only reason why, in the artistic reaches of semantics, our age lacks the greatness that some of its predecessors have attained.

Individual words have lost the magic and black magic powers that men once thought to conjure with; and what humanistic glamour can be mustered into modern slogans is soon dispelled by the omnipresent resistance to propaganda. Proverbs are going out of style, having proved one of the most obstinate elements of folk culture in the face of ineluctable social change and world orientation.

Allegories strike us as a stale and unappealing resource. Yet this class holds some great symbols that have outlived much marble and bronze: Plato's myth of the cave, the ingenious expression of an abstract epistemology, and his myth of the charioteer driving two horses, the one docile and the other recalcitrant, an ever fresh picture of his doctrine of the tripartite soul. Many of Jesus' parables have converted abstractions into *idées-forces* capable of molding the lives of men. Perhaps allegory is not dead yet.

Religious architecture and civil architecture as the symbol of civic loyalties would contribute to our repertory of great models; and likewise religious ritual, with such refinements as the universal *autos sacramentales* of a Calderón.

Institutions may not be too abstract to serve as symbols. The United Nations, Unesco, and Unesco's sister agencies symbolize perhaps more aptly than any finished work of art the common aspiration and common effort which are all we have, in the mid-twentieth century, of a world community.

But this will suffice for you to imagine what I mean by finding symbols for the vital ideas of our time.

Does it claim too much, in such a time of deep-reaching crisis in human affairs, to speak of the humanities as the very *basis* of community among peoples? I would answer "No"—provided that creative scholars and creative artists can bring to the ailing world the requisite knowledge, the requisite experience, and the requisite symbolic expression of the common human values that lie submerged in the minds of men.

11 The Fine Arts as a Humanistic Study

Wolfgang Stechow

As pointed out by our moderator, we are here to elaborate the "meaning of the fine arts for the intellectual and emotional development of the individual living in a democracy."

I should like to comment first on the dual implied by the words "intellectual *and* emotional development of the individual." One of the most serious obstacles on the road to grasping the real meaning of art has been the unwarranted and disastrous war between factions monopolizing the intellectual *or* the emotional aspects of art respectively, a dichotomy which, to make things worse, has often been confused with the friction between modern art and art of the past, between form and content and what have you. All this assorted confusion has resulted in thoroughly troubled waters in which cheap popularizers have been doing some excellent fishing.

He who feels nothing when looking at a great work of art, whether ancient, medieval, Renaissance, or modern, is no guide to the fine arts as a humanistic study. But the same is true of him who does not go beyond telling his students or readers that such masterpieces are "somehow," by the grace of something vague often called "creativeness," great works of art. If the *intellectual* aspect is totally ignored, the student falls easy prey to the slogan of the mystic remoteness and aloofness of art and the

artist, to cheap anti-intellectualism, uncritical disciple-
ship, and eventually, after this has worn out, to complete
cynicism and skepticism. If the *emotional* aspect is totally
ignored, the student falls easy prey to mere formalism
and hyperintellectualism, and eventually, after this has
worn out, likewise to complete cynicism and skepticism.
However, it is hardly doubtful that the dangers inherent
in a one-sidedly emotional, anti-intellectual approach are
more frequently in evidence and more consistently over-
looked by many writers on art than are the dangers
inherent in an overintellectual approach. The danger inherent in a one-sidedly emotional approach is most readily
understood when we consider the role of subject matter
per se. The uninformed can be very easily persuaded that
any picture representing the salute to the flag or any por-
trait of Lenin is great regardless of its merits as a work of
art. To some degree, the same is true of a still life which
evokes an appetite for an orange, a landscape "in which
one would like to build a house," or a nude which has all
it takes. But the uninformed can also be easily persuaded
that an abstraction is great regardless of its merits as a
work of art, because abstraction, either as the *dernier cri*
or for more valid reasons, may exert a purely emotional
appeal. A humanistic approach, however, involves by definition the power and use of reasoning, reasoning not
only with regard to subject matter but also with regard to
form. For great art, though originating in the realm of
intuition and the infinite, is incarnated in form, and form
is finite and concrete, that is, human, and open to reasoned
analysis. This also implies that there is no such thing as
bringing art down to the human level, but only an ele-
vating of art to the human level, since mystic vagueness is

surely not to be considered as a superhuman level. A humanistic approach to art therefore involves familiarity with many other aspects which are indissolubly connected with the human realm, such as technical problems, problems of individual interpretation, and, generally, with the sociological and historical context—all thoroughly human matters. It is here that the aspect of the "individual living in a democracy" enters as a decisive factor. It behooves an individual living in a democratic society, that is, an individual interested as much in problems as he is in solutions, to weigh, inquire, deliberate in order to arrive at a reasoned conviction, and to match enthusiasm with understanding. Speaking from the point of view of an enlightened democratic society, then, one might say that art has too long been granted an exceptional position which has brought little more than embarrassment and ambiguity to the cause of art and the artist. Too long has the fallacy been allowed to prevail that in the realm of the beautiful, the criteria employed in the realms of the true and the just have no validity. Truth and justice, too, partake in the realm of intuition and the infinite, but they have become part of our world in the concrete terms of research and law. They, too, cannot exist without our *feeling* strongly about them; they, too, cannot work without our *understanding* them. There is no earthly reason why the realm of the beautiful should be exempt from the same considerations. And just as we believe that truth and justice are best taken care of in a democracy, that is, in terms of affection enlightened by critical understanding, the realm of the beautiful, in its widest sense, will best be taken care of in a democracy, that is, in terms of affection enlightened by critical understanding. But this can be achieved only under two conditions: (1) that our concept of these realms keeps developing, and (2) that this development is borne by independent individuals who know what they are talking and writing about. Let us consider, in conclusion, a few aspects of these two *sine qua nons*.

Development excludes static adherence to fixed concepts as to what is beautiful. Nearly 450 years ago, one of the greatest artists of all time who was also one of the greatest thinkers on art of all time, Albrecht Dürer, said: "What beauty is, I know not"; but he also said: "Now, since we cannot attain to the very best, shall we give up our research altogether? This beastly thought we do not accept." His never contented but never resigned striving for an enlightened concept of beauty has outlasted hundreds of water-tight systems of aesthetics because it allowed for the *development* in concepts of art. But what would we know about the creed of Albrecht Dürer, or, for that matter, of the similarly broad-minded creeds of Rubens and Cézanne, of Mozart and Schumann, of Montaigne and Goethe, or of non-artists like Erasmus of Rotterdam and Jakob Burckhardt, if we had considered art-historical research as the antiquarian waste of time which many artists and writers on art have seen in it, or if we had restricted our interpretation of art to an effort to see our own little likes and dislikes vindicated by it? Intelligent, unbiased investigation of all aspects of the history of art alone can guarantee the understanding of the essentials of the development in artistic views and the resulting realization of such views in the great works of art themselves. In order to achieve this, we must bend all our efforts upon the establishment of art courses in our colleges and universities in which the aspects of change in

artistic expression are recognized as a *sine qua non* for a
real understanding of art. Average "appreciation" courses,
water-tight systems of aesthetics, indoctrination, disciple-
making simply will not do. Naturally, a mere lining up of
facts of art history will not do either; the job asks for an
historical sense which involves more problems than solutions, more looking and listening and reading than talking.

This brings us to the second of our *sine qua nons:* the
independent individual to whose hands such a task must
be entrusted. The success of this kind of teaching depends entirely on how it is done, not on blueprints, catalogue descriptions, and textbooks. Also, it depends on
knowledge, not on good intentions. Furthermore, that
individual must himself be the object, and subject, of a
development which, in turn, depends on his continued
activity as a critical reader, listener, traveler, and writer.
Unless we provide for the training of such teachers, and,
through them, for the instruction of a new generation in
"Fine Arts as a Humanistic Study," we shall betray our
democratic ideals with regard to a subject of ever increasing importance, a subject endowed with an infinite
capacity to enrich the lives of all future generations.

Serge Chermayeff

In an industrial society such as ours in which we rely more and more on specialists and machines to produce the various control and communication instruments, the creative act or experience becomes progressively more and more remote to the average individual: we are living in a society in which spectators and consumers are the majority, the creative individual a shrinking minority. The probability of transference of creative experience will become negligible if we cannot find new means of counteracting the anti-art development inherent in a laissez-faire industrial civilization.

The high level of sensibility which can produce art or the appreciation of it is the product of integration of a well-developed sensuality—oral, visual, tactile—with intelligence. Does our society tend to develop this kind of integrated individual? The evidence seems to point to the contrary: we are actually inhibiting the very qualities which we need for the development of a contemporary art commensurate with contemporary science and technology. In the realm of economics, politics, philosophy, and art—these areas of human activity which have many intangibles—we have deliberately ignored demonstrable facts. We have gone out of our way to obscure or distort these facts with a curtain of meaningless words. We have gloried in self-deception which would not be tolerated for a moment in matters of technology, science, or business.

The majority of our citizens look with their ears and

hear with their eyes, or have developed the capacity to be quite blind or deaf to anything they find difficult or distasteful. Civilized man accepts unquestioningly prescriptions and definitions of others on matters about which he should have firsthand intellectual and sensual reactions of his own. He looks at labels and accepts values established all too often with the mortician's yardstick in our museums, but he does not *see* architecture, painting, and sculpture. He responds to pecuniary values of objects, but cannot respond to their form or, in applied arts, cannot have a clear view of their usefulness. Most of our citizens, day in and day out, on the one hand pass, unseeingly and unmoved, the obsolete, hideous and monstrous things which crowd our homes, our streets, our cities, and which threaten to spread like a fog to engulf and destroy our countryside and darken the sunlight. On the other hand, we pass equally unseeingly the new, often vital and exciting things which are natural instruments with which to create a new order.

If what I have outlined is even partially true, and I do not think I have exaggerated observable facts, do we not have to ask ourselves if a society which on the whole inhibits the very attributes which are essential to good health can hope to achieve the goals we have set ourselves without a drastic and widespread program of social therapy?

I am convinced that a creative experience is a major instrument in such a therapeutic treatment. It will be necessary in the first place to change radically our prevailing attitude toward art. Art must cease being considered as a commodity provided by mysteriously endowed specialists for the delectation of an equally exclusive body of patrons and must become an activity in which all participate. Then art can become an instrument of social therapy as potent as security and health.

The form of education which we adopt at this time will determine to a large extent whether the process of inhibition leading to atrophy of our essential sensual equipment will continue or will stop, whether the veils before our eyes will be torn away and we will see that which is living and real. If our concept of education is not based upon the joining of emotion and intellect in all action at the highest level of which we are capable, the result will be the very antithesis of the high purpose which we profess.

Is it not necessary to begin working toward building a physical environment consonant with our aspirations and productive potential? We will have gone far toward the achievement of our educational objectives in their widest sense when we have established a sense of security based upon the four freedoms and have implemented these concepts with the physical fact of good housing and schools, well-planned cities, and preserved natural resources.

13 The Function of Art in the Human Economy

T HERE is one question which in our day is of fundamental interest to the student of aesthetics in regard to art: the function that it performs in the human economy. Until the end of the eighteenth century, more or less, the answer which was universally accepted was that given by Aristotle in the *Poetics* to the effect that the function of art is imitation. If one asked why men are interested in imitation, the answer was that imitation is an activity natural to man and that it is natural to delight in works of imitation. The revolution at the beginning of the modern age that dethroned Aristotle from the place given him by Saint Thomas had left intact his primacy in aesthetics, and the modern age had to wait till the German romantics to rid itself of the Aristotelian hegemony in aesthetics.

That the theory of imitation was accepted for so long is no proof of its truth but is, at least, an indication of its utility. However, the usefulness and even the truth the theory had for the fine arts had considerably diminished by the middle of the nineteenth century, and thus we find Delacroix concerned in his *Journals*, in the entries made after 1850, with the relation of the object of imitation to the product of his brush; for, as he puts it, unless the artist mixes something of himself with the feelings that come from the object that strikes him, they do not please. Delacroix does not fall back on the word *expression*, as we do today, to convey what he means, but it is not difficult to see that it was toward the expression theory that he was groping in his *Journals*. Delacroix does not deny that the artist imitates and that part of the appeal of art resides in the recognition of the imitated object; but he is fairly clear that the appeal of imitation is to a certain part of the intelligence, and that the main appeal of art is to be found in the fact that painted objects are, as he puts it, "like a solid bridge on which the imagination supports itself to penetrate to the mysterious and profound sensation for which the forms are, so to speak, the hieroglyph, but a hieroglyph far more eloquent than a cold representation."

We cannot expect of a painter a rigorously philosophical development of his views. But for my purpose this is no obstacle, since it was not till the end of the nineteenth century that the expression theory was formulated by aestheticians. And the first question to which I should like to address myself is whether this theory is capable of explaining satisfactorily the function that art performs in the human economy.

I do not mean to deny the utility to which the great success of the expression theory points. Since the middle of the nineteenth century painters have been trying to liberate themselves from slavery to the model and the theory of expression in its several variants has justified these efforts. It gave the artist freedom to look beyond the conventional, realistic appearance of objects to many of their structural aspects which until then had been noticed only incidentally, and it allowed him to look also within himself and to put on canvas what he thought he found there. Nor is the expression theory merely useful; it has in it at least as much of the truth as the imitation theory. For if the artist must finally go to nature for his forms, with the Germans and with Coleridge it must be admitted that he is also *creative*—in the sense that he adds something out of the spontaneity of his mind to what he gathers through his experience, and this addition is an "expression," a pressing-out of his inward resources, and hence an authentic sign of what essentially he is and, in so far as he is representative of his people and day, of what they are.

However, although one ought to grant a modicum of truth to the expression theory, I cannot convince myself that the importance that art has in the human economy derives merely from the fact that it allows the artist to express himself. For what is it that he expresses? Usually it is assumed that he expresses his emotions. And if this is the interpretation that we must put on the theory, it is difficult to guess what can be meant by expressing on canvas an emotion by the means employed by the painter —unless the word "express" be used to signify that through the grasp of certain causal relations and conventional associations between, on the one hand, the object painted and the means used to paint it and, on the other hand, the spectator the painter is able to arouse a constellation of emotions in the spectator. If this is what is meant by "expression" one must observe that it certainly cannot be proved that the painter is always able to control by means of his finished canvas the emotion he wishes to arouse, even in those who look at his work with full cognizance of the conventions which he uses. On this point I believe that we have abundant empirical evidence, gathered by psychologists under conditions which meet scientific demands. But even if this could not be demonstrated inductively it is not obvious how art can derive the importance that it has in human culture from the fact that it enables the artist to manipulate his public emotionally with a certain precision.

If one went on to add that the arousal of emotion was cathartic, one could make something of the expression theory. This would trace the importance of art to its therapeutic function; but we know how very doubtful and ambiguous theories of catharsis are, from the earliest Aristotelian form of the theory to the new-fangled formulation which I. A. Richards has given it. Nor do I believe that it is catharsis which the expression theory usually intends. In any case it does not seem to me to have been shown convincingly that the arousal of emotion has the cathartic effect that this interpretation of it would claim for it. It is true that in hospitals music is beginning to be used successfully for medical purposes; and if painting is used in hospitals not occupationally but for the therapeutic effects of its character as painting in the same sense that music is, I doubt that this use could adequately account for its importance in the life of the normal man.

But let us look into the theory that the function of art is to purge us of the emotions it arouses in us. First, it assumes that the emotion, like the humors of Ben Johnson's comedies, are somehow stored up in the psyche, waiting to be aroused and drained. But this is a very coarse conception of emotion. The tensions, the frustrations and bafflements, the malice and fear which poison men morally are not fluids that are stored up and can be drained off through their arousal. But even if they were, even if the theory were more than bad science for which there is no evidence, something would happen to art were we to endow it with dignity because of its medicinal utility. Had the function of art been to imitate, when the camera was discovered it would have done away with the need for the painter—as indeed in the eyes of the ignorant it has already done—since the camera can do the work of imitation more faithfully and more cheaply than the painter can. Similarly, if the function of art is to purge the emotions, the day will surely come when men will have the sense to turn to psychiatrists who will undoubtedly more completely and more effectively relieve them of their psychic ills than Picasso ever could.

But the function of art is not to arouse and purge the emotions. It does arouse emotion, but only incidentally, and certainly the position that it occupies in the economy of life cannot be attributed to the fact that it does. What the artist does is to create and in the act of creation to discover—and I intend seriously to maintain this seeming paradox—the structure of reality as it reveals itself to him through his eyes. Thus his is as cognitive a task as that of the physicist, although the knowledge he gives us, thank God, does not lead us to increase our power over nature. There are other important differences, for the knowledge that the artist gives us is knowledge of the primary data of experience which the artist organizes for us and presents to our apprehension in terms of structures and media that satisfy our craving for axiological no less than mathematical rationality. Nor is the knowl-

edge, therefore, verifiable as the physicist's is. Nor is it
deeper, nor is the reality that the painter offers us any
more real than that of the physicist—it is merely of a
different order.

Thus art has to do with the metaphysical nature of
man, even if, by putting it in these terms, one is certain
that the statement will not be understood by the positivistic mentality of the technological man of our day.
But perhaps I should not say that art has to do with the
metaphysical nature of man, and not because the natural-
ists cannot understand the statement, but because it is
not altogether true, since what art does by revealing as it
creates the structure of reality which presents itself to the
artist through his eyes is to inform the animal with humanity, to make him a man, a human being, enabling
him thus to transcend his biological heritage; in short, to
enable him to snatch at the spirituality that would otherwise escape him.

Hence the tremendous importance of art, although in
an age drunken with technological power and misguided
by bad philosophy, as ours is, what I have claimed for
art is likely to be taken for mystical twaddle. Let me
therefore stop a minute to translate what I have just said
into different terms in an effort to make it a little more
plausible.

Let me begin by reminding you of a statement made by
Boas in his book on primitive art. Boas points out that
there are no people known to the anthropologist, no matter
how close to the level of mere survival, that do not put into
art energies that they can ill afford to subtract from their
struggle against nature. If the business of man were sur-

vival or pleasure or secular happiness, if man were not a metaphysical animal in all the senses of this richly ambiguous word, the expenditure of energy on art by primitive peoples would be wanton waste. For art demands talent and time and physical energy; it demands materials which must be procured with labor and the development of specialized skills which drain the strength of a group.

Men can bring themselves to full human completion with but little technology, with no positive science of the kind that we Westerners have developed, and certainly—and I cannot say this with anything but regret—even without any philosophy whatever. But without religion and without art they cannot do it. I do not mean, of course, that individuals cannot, for those living in a culture rich in spiritual values can live dedicated exclusively to utilitarian and hedonic ends and yet remain human without art and without myth. I mean that taken collectively men cannot hope to survive as human beings without these agencies.

What the artist does, then, is to organize the primary data of experience, providing us thus with the elements of rationality. He is not the only one who performs this most important of tasks. But the complexity of reality would overwhelm us if we had to achieve rationality without the aid of art. One could live without art—one can live without eyes and multiply biologically, as blind fish and moles do. But one cannot come to full human awareness without eyes—and without awareness a man is a mere animal. However, when eyes are used merely for the grasp of signs, to supply the stimulus to our practical responses, the values which dwell upon the colorful structure of the visible world are lost to us. For on the view I am defending the values are not projections of impulses or characters objectified by interests but discoveries, as real and as objective as are the habits of nature which it is the business of the physicist to formulate into laws.

The comparison with the habits of nature enables me to elucidate, to some extent at least, the paradox I flatly stated some pages back, when I said that the artist both creates and discovers the structure of reality. For it is proper to say that the scientist discovers the laws of nature. But if we try to state more precisely what he does, we shall see that he discovers the habits of nature which he formulates into laws. The habits are there prior to his search for them. But the laws into which the scientist formulates these habits are somewhat artificial, being a statement which depends not only on the habits that are there to be discovered but on the means at the command of the scientist at the time of the discovery and on the happy gift of creativity that he has in formulating his discoveries elegantly, economically, and systematically. Similarly with the creative artist: he discovers the axio-logical structure of reality that his dominant sense leads him to search for, but this value-freighted reality and its structure are there before he learns to paint or carve. But what he discovers he creates, as we say, in that he utters it through the medium and the manner of his art, and in painting the manner and to some extent the me-dium are artificial and conventional and therefore vary from culture to culture, from age to age, and even from individual to individual; so that what is fully before the eyes is always in a degree idiosyncratic and always to a great extent conventional; and yet the structure of the visible world exhibited by the artist is as much a part of reality as are the laws of nature which the physicist discovers. It is through the apprehension of these structures, in art no less than in science, that we fulfill our destiny. For the end of man is to become human, and this is something which he does by developing his soul through art, religion, science, and philosophy, by seeking the best knowledge, which is the knowledge of the eternal.

14 The Divorce of Music and Learning

Donald J. Grout

An issue that ought to concern us in a symposium on the humanities in American society may be stated thus: "Is the study of music a proper part of a humanistic education?" If for the time being you will be kind enough to grant the possibility of an affirmative answer to this question, I will go on to ask another: "What kind of study of music would have relevance in such a program?"

The necessity for this question rises from a peculiarity in the nature of music itself, or at least in the nature of musical practice. It is well known that to all studies there is prerequisite a certain degree of technical competence in handling the material: before you can study a literature, for example, you must learn to read the language in which it is written; in studying mathematics you must learn to draw mathematical symbols. I am not aware that teachers of English literature generally expect their students to develop the ability to declaim Shakespeare's lines with all the vocal color, nuances, gestures, and facial expressions of a finished actor. Neither do I understand that teachers of geometry as a rule value very highly the ability on the part of a student to draw the lines of geometrical figures in a skillful manner if it appears that the student does not know what he is drawing or cannot demonstrate the geometrical relationships existing between the parts of the figure. In other words, the essence of the subject in both these cases consists not in the ability to produce in sensuously agreeable form the symbols of the ideas, but in understanding the ideas themselves. In fact, I take it to be one mark of humanistic education, as distinct from professional training, that in the former the attention is devoted to contemplation rather than manipulation, that one's concern is (to use Lord Bacon's antithesis) with Wisdom rather than Power. [1]

Now for all the fine arts the sensuous quality of the materials is a matter of great importance; in this respect the fine arts may be said to stand at one extreme of a scale, of which mathematics stands at the other extreme and literature (particularly poetry) somewhere between. And it happens that among the fine arts the materials of music are, in the opinion of many people, the most elusive, complex, mysterious, and difficult to master. From this opinion arises the common confusion we hear illustrated nearly every time a person says, "I am studying music." What he usually means, and what his hearers usually understand him to mean, is that he is engaged in perfecting his skill at manipulating some kind of instrument for the purpose of producing musical sounds. Such an aim, it is true, may be pursued for many years of devoted labor before anything like perfection is reached; and anyone who has undergone this discipline may perhaps be forgiven for believing that what he has done constitutes "the" study of music. But really it is as if one were to say, "I am studying English literature," when in fact he is cultivating his voice so as to pronounce words and sentences in as pleasing a manner as possible; or as if one were to say, "I am studying geometry," when he is in fact learning to draw polygons and circles as accurately,

[1] Francis Bacon, *Of the Advancement of Learning*, Book I.

easily, and beautifully as possible. It is, in short, a confusion between learning to manipulate material and understanding the ideas expressed or embodied in the material. And the fact that in the case of music the confusion is so widespread and generally unrealized should not prevent our seeing that it is a confusion nevertheless.

One of its consequences is this peculiar idea of what constitutes musical education, to which I have already alluded. No one will deny the need for musical performance, since in this art the performer is the essential medium without whom the composer's intentions cannot be realized. But to stop at that point is surely to miss something. I once heard the dean of one of the largest music schools in this country say in a public address, quite casually as if it were a matter of common acceptance, "Of course we are all gratified when we see one of our students at the pinnacle of success, singing on the stage of the Metropolitan Opera or giving a successful concert in Carnegie Hall." Naturally any of us would be gratified under such circumstances; but why we should regard them as exemplifying the supreme goal of education in music I do not understand. Of course it will be pointed out that one cannot perform a work of music without in some sense "understanding" it, and with this I agree; but this is not the kind of understanding I am talking about, nor is it a kind of understanding that seems to have a very direct bearing on humanistic values in education.

Another consequence—and at the same time partly a cause—of our confusion about the true nature of the study of music appears in the most diverse and charming guises if we contemplate the attitudes people commonly have toward musicians. These range from casual contempt to rapt adoration, but one thing is common to them all: the musician is thought of as a creature set apart from common humanity—as either an eccentric or a god, as either someone to be regarded with that mixture of pity and aversion people feel for the mentally unfortunate or someone to be worshipped, but never quite as a normal being with a rational mind. The sacred academic name of "professor" is often taken in vain by being applied to barroom pianists and leaders of vaudeville theater orchestras; but between the state of mind that finds this sort of thing humorous and the state of mind of a sophomore listening to Dizzie Gillespie, or the state of mind of an aesthetically susceptible female at a Stokowsky concert, the difference is usually negligible. Nor do musicians as a rule meet with much more intelligent appreciation from either the poets or the historians. Even university faculties, I suspect, do not feel quite easy unless the musicians are safely penned in an academic stockade known as The School of Music, and any gestures from within looking like preparations for a foray into broader academic pastures are likely to be viewed with incredulity and some polite dismay by custodians of the good old Liberal Arts tradition. In a word, the musicians find themselves pretty thoroughly cut off from the established intellectual life of our tir :; and too often their physical nearness on the campus only emphasizes their loneliness.

I suppose most of us would agree that this is unfortunate. It seems to me that the blame for it can be placed about equally on two false doctrines: first, on the one-sided view of music already mentioned, which concentrates on the manipulative and physical factors at the expense of the intellectual; and second, on an opposite but equally dangerous narrow view of music to which we shall now turn our attention, namely a view that regards this art as if it existed in a sociological and historical vacuum, owing nothing to the life surrounding it. These two errors I shall call respectively the error of attachment and the error of detachment; attachment too exclusively to the sensuous material and detachment from the concerns of life as a whole. Their historical origins seem fairly plain. The error of attachment begins in the sixteenth century, when for the first time we hear of virtuosi who are admired for nothing except their virtuosity. The error of detachment seems to date from about the same period. But whatever their origins, that these errors are perpetuated is the fault of our schools and departments of music; and unless we correct them I cannot see that we have a very strong case for music as subject matter in a program of humanistic education.

We may appropriately speak of the "divorce" of music and learning, for the two were once joined. Everyone knows that music formed one division of the quadrivium in the medieval system of studies. During the late Middle Ages Oxford and the German universities required music as part of the complete curriculum.[2] Degrees were offered in music at Salamanca from the fourteenth century, and at both Oxford and Cambridge from the fifteenth century.[3] Exactly what constituted the study of music in the Middle

[2] Hastings Rashdall, *The Universities of Europe in the Middle Ages* (Oxford, 1895), I:441.
[3] *Ibid.*, II:75, 458.

Ages and in the earliest universities is not altogether clear, but as far as we can judge from the treatises of medieval writers on the subject it consisted for the largest part of a mixture of what we would now call acoustics and music theory. However, this was not the whole story. In the earliest teachings, and especially in the writings of Boethius, music was defined in terms that obviously imply a much wider scope for the subject than we are today accustomed to admit. Boethius (d. *ca.* 524) is important to us because it was he who laid the foundations for the entire medieval view of music; all later writers on music copied from him, and his text was still prescribed in universities in the fifteenth century. According to one of these later writers,[4] Boethius defined music as "the investigation and classification ... of concord and consonance existing among opposite and dissimilar things brought together in unity." Boethius also, following ancient authors, makes the familiar threefold division of music into *mundana, humana, organica,* that is to say, the harmony of the cosmos, the harmony of the soul with the body, and lastly the artificial harmony which man makes with voices and instruments. In the light of such a comprehensive view of the subject we may understand

---

[4] Abbot Engelbert Admotensis (1297–1331), *De musica*, in Gerbert, *Scriptores ecclesiastici de musica sacra potissimum* (Milan, 1931), II:288: *Musica generaliter sumendo est scientia inquirendi et discernendi secundum proportiones harmonicas, concordantiam et consonatiam in contrariis et dissimilibus rebus sibi coniunctis aut collatis. Haec descriptio colligitur ex verbis Boetii de Musica libro I, capitulo 19.* This definition is not found in so many words in Boethius, but it can legitimately be inferred from what he writes, particularly in the first two chapters of his first Book. The exact wording is not important for our purpose, since we are at least as much concerned with what later medieval writers thought Boethius said as with what he actually did say.

what Isidore of Seville (d. 636) meant by saying that *sine musica nulla disciplina potest esse perfecta.*[5] Practically all subsequent medieval writers on music acknowledge, at least in theory and with expressions of respect, the fundamental views of Boethius. Now I suggest that it is not merely coincidence that during all the thousand years when music was regularly regarded as one of the seven liberal arts within the whole body of recognized higher learning music was also regarded as a science whose bounds extended to the outermost limits of the universe, as a principle of order which was illustrated whenever opposites were held together in unity, and what we now call music was thought to be no more than an imperfect imitation or copy of the harmony of the spheres in their courses or that subtler harmony by virtue of which body and soul were joined in one being. Please do not understand me as advocating a return to medieval cosmology or scholastic metaphysics. All I am saying is that in the Middle Ages teachers of music believed their subject to have a quite clearly defined relation to human and cosmic affairs. Whether or not they were correct in their views as to the nature of that relation is beside the point. The point is that they believed it to exist.

When we come to the end of the sixteenth century we

[5] *Etymologarum sive originum libri xx*, ed. W. M. Lindsay (Oxford, s.d.), Lib. III, xviii. *Cf.* also Johannes de Muris in the fourteenth century (Gerbert, *Scriptores*, III:285): *Musica est ars artium domina, continens omnia principia methodorum, in primo certitudinus (gradu) confirmata, in natura rerum omnium modo mirabili proportionaliter internata, delectabilis intellectu, amabilis in auditu, tristes laetificans, avaros amplificans,*—and many other useful things; but note the low place of *amabilis in auditu* in the listing!

find that the situation has changed. Thomas Morley in the preface of his *Plaine and Easie Introduction to Practicall Musicke* (1597) frankly says, "And as for the definition, division, partes, and kindes of Musicke, I have omitted them as things only serving to content the learned, and not for the instruction of the ignorant." Not quite two hundred years later the extreme reaction against the doctrines of Boethius may be seen in Charles Burney's definition of music as "an innocent luxury, unnecessary, indeed, to our existence, but a great improvement and gratification of the sense of hearing."[6] In short, as we move historically from the Renaissance toward our own day we find two processes going on: the materials and forms of music are growing more and more complex and diverse, and the art is reaching out to wider and wider audiences; at the same time musicians, more and more fascinated by the material of their art and the ever increasing possibilities of its manipulation, forgetting the ancient conception of the wholeness of music within the intellectual life of man and turning Narcissus-like to the contemplation of their own lineaments, become content to think of their art no longer as a corporeal image of the harmony of the universe, but as "an innocent luxury." No doubt many musicians even of the late eighteenth century would have deprecated the extreme wording of Dr. Burney's statement; and his words obviously do not apply to a composer like J. S. Bach, for whom, incidentally, Burney had little understanding. The nineteenth century is full of attempts by musicians to close the gap between music and life,

[6] Charles Burney, *A General History of Music*, Vol. I (1776), first "Definition."

including the grandiose but historically futile *Gesamtkunstwerk* theory of Wagner. That this and like efforts failed to inherit the earth may perhaps be ascribed to a certain noticeable lack of meekness on the part of their propagators.

At any rate, music by the end of the nineteenth century was still not generally regarded as a mirror of the universe in the Boethian sense; it was still a luxury, though possibly a less innocent one than in Dr. Burney's time. And again I suggest that it may not be merely coincidence that during the time when music had lost the ancient sense of oneness with the whole of human learning and had become almost completely absorbed in its own bodily elements and sensations, it ceased to be accepted as one of the liberal arts and its teaching passed almost completely out of the universities into technical schools and conservatories. The return began in the second half of the nineteenth century with the establishment of chairs of musicology in some of the German universities. The movement has continued to a limited degree in our own country with the establishment of departments of music in the liberal arts colleges and schools of music in the universities. But the breach is still far from being healed. Music and learning do live together on many of our campuses, but there is an uneasy feeling that they are living in sin and not in lawful wedlock. The impediments to a remarriage are the two errors I have mentioned. These impediments are to be removed, if at all, through the mediation of the scholar-musician, or musician-scholar, whichever term you prefer. And I should like to devote the remainder of this paper to considering two questions: (1) Under what conditions can the musician-scholar effectively work, and (2) what sort of person ought he to be?

I think the first condition is that there be a revision of the common attitude about the principal aim of studying music. We must take a clear distinction between the professional training of musicians on the one hand and education in music on the other. This means, I believe, that if a school or department of music is to make any real move in the direction of being a place for educating people, its policies must be under the direction of the scholar, not the composer or the performer. This is not to say that the teaching of musical performance is to be abolished; on the contrary, it is to be fostered as part of that mastery of the technical material of the subject which is a necessary prerequisite to scholarship. But technical mastery is not to be regarded as an end in itself, or as anything other than a means toward the more inclusive goal of understanding the material with which the study of music is properly concerned. In other words, we must expel that false doctrine which I have called the error of attachment.

In the second place, we must recover a sense of the wholeness of human life, and of music as a part of that life. If the error of attachment has proceeded from the side of the practitioners of music, it must be confessed that the opposite error of detachment has proceeded from the scholars as well as the practitioners. You may read many a history of music without ever suspecting that the successive changes of musical style and forms had any but the most superficial connection with goings-on in the rest of the world in which the composers lived. The never-never land of the old-fashioned music historian was populated by strange abstractions which behaved in the most unaccountable ways. The ricercare, for example, by some mysterious parturition "gave birth" to the fugue; the French overture and the Italian overture "struggled for mastery" and the latter, for no particularly convincing reason, won out. We are now beginning to emerge from this primitive, animistic stage in the study of music, but we still have a long way to go before we fashion a theory of the connection between music and the rest of life that will be as satisfying to us as the theory of Boethius was to the Middle Ages. Obviously there is no question of our going back to actual medieval beliefs about music. What we need is a modern equivalent of that which lay behind the medieval beliefs, namely the conviction of the oneness of all knowledge and a vision of the infinitely diverse implications of the ideas in a subject like music. Our mode of realizing these things will, of course, be different from the mode in which Boethius realized them; we shall approach the problem not exclusively through metaphysics, but through historical, sociological, and other methods as well. Along with the necessary work of minute research there must be serious study of all the phenomena of music in our whole culture, and scholars who undertake such study must try to overcome their habitual timidity and have the courage to propound hypotheses, taking the usual risk that their hypotheses may be replaced by better ones as knowledge advances.

This outline of the conditions requisite for the musician-scholar's work has partly anticipated the answer to our question about that person's qualifications. Briefly, they are that he should be competent to carry out the removal of the two errors of attachment and detachment that now stand in the way of the acceptance of music as a humanistic study. It is, I believe, fairly common for the so-called practical musicians to assume that musicologists are mere theorists. I can only say that so far as my own experience goes, all the good musicologists whom I know are also good musicians; most of them have had some period of rigorous professional training in musical technique of one sort or another, and not a few of them are very competent players or conductors. In fact, I think it is not going too far to say that some such competence and some experience under really exacting conditions of the actual business of making music are an indispensable part of a music scholar's training. Unless he has gone through the stages of mastering the material for himself, it is doubtful that he can ever have a really inward comprehension of music, especially in its historical development, where so many issues turn on the problems of musical performance. But musicianship is not enough. The demands of scholarship are equally exacting. Scholarship in music cannot afford to be one whit less thorough than in any other field of learning whatsoever. A competent music scholar must have had a standard classical education, must be well acquainted with modern literature, must know his history, be something of a physicist, psychologist, philosopher, and anthropologist, must be able to read at least six languages, know how to use the tools of bibliography, and have in his mind a comprehensive idea of the important works of published research in his own field. Along with all this he must never cease to be a musician. If his learning ever stifles his sensitiveness to beauty, he is lost. This necessary balance of aesthetic sensibility, analytical penetration, and scholarly technique is the peculiar requirement for the scholar whose subject is the fine arts. He is truly, in the Boethian phrase, a "concord and consonance existing among opposite and dissimilar things brought together."

And now, by way of exemplifying what is called in musical analysis three-part (or A B A) form, let me revert to the question with which this paper began: is the study of music a proper part of a humanistic education? I think the answer is, "Yes, if—": if, that is, the study of music can rid itself of the two errors which still so largely beset it, namely the error of a too exclusive attachment to the physical material with neglect of the intellectual content and the error of detachment of the subject matter of music from the whole body of learning. And these two errors can be overcome, it seems to me, through the agency of the musician-scholar.

Since we are concerned in this symposium with the general subject of the humanities, it would seem appropriate to conclude this paper by reference to a humanist of the Renaissance, one who is regarded by many as the greatest of all the humanists, Angelo Ambrogini, known as Poliziano, who lived from 1454 to 1494 and worked at the court of Lorenzo the Magnificent in Florence. I consider Poliziano to be worthy of emulation not because he was particularly learned in music, but because he seems to me to be an ideal type of scholar whose subject is the artistic productions of human genius. In his case, the particular subject was the literature of ancient Greece and Rome. Consider his qualifications as a scholar: in the first place, he was himself a poet in the Latin tongue. He knew the

material of his subject not merely through acquaintance
with the productions of others but through having worked
with that material himself. In the second place, he did
not restrict his interest to what we should now call "high-
brow" literature (which in his time meant exclusively
ancient Greek and Roman authors), but wrote also in
the language of the people, imitating and glorifying the
forms of Tuscan popular poetry of his day. In the third
place he was not blind to the links between his own art
and the other arts; his *Orfeo* (produced at Mantua some-
time between 1472 and 1483) is a true lyrical drama, in-
terspersing the spoken poetry with songs, choruses, and
instrumental music; and although there is no proof, it is
not unlikely that Poliziano himself had at least some share
in the selection or even the composition of the music. In
the fourth place, as a scholar, Poliziano's learning is said
to have been prodigious. His method of teaching is not
without suggestiveness for teachers of music today:

> It was the method of professors of that period to
> read the Greek and Latin authors with their class,
> dictating philological and critical notes, emending
> corrupt passages in the received texts, offering
> elucidations of the matter, and pouring forth
> stores of acquired knowledge regarding the laws,
> manners, religious and philosophical opinions of
> the ancients.[7]

Finally, Poliziano is to be praised and emulated because his learning was so conceived and executed as to
be itself a work of art not unworthy of comparison with

[7] J. A. Symonds, "Politian," in *Encyclopaedia Britannica* (11th ed.).

those greater works of art which formed the subject of his studies. Of all productions of scholarship, those that deal with beautiful objects should most aspire to be beautiful in themselves; to exemplify not merely the scholar, but the scholar as artist, one who aims to merit the description Symonds applies to Poliziano:[8] "He must have acquired the erudition of his eminently learned century. . . . Moreover, he must be strong enough to carry this erudition without bending beneath its weight; dexterous enough to use it without pedantry; exuberant enough in natural resources to reduce his stores of learning . . . to one ruling harmony," and above all "gifted with [a] reverent sense of beauty."

[8] J. A. Symonds, *The Renaissance in Italy: Italian Literature* (New York, 1882–83), I:400.

15 Music and the Listening Audience

Rudolf Kolisch

IN MY contribution to this discussion I should like to present a problem which is basic to the consideration of music as a part of the humanistic tradition. Obviously, the first step in the preservation of music as a humane study lies in making it an integral part of the background of the educated man. But how is this to come about? For today every possible outlet for great music has been so debased by the monopolistic control of music distribution in this country, that is, by the music industry, that music has been degraded from an art into a mere product of business, the public concert has become a potpourri of the popular in which the great works of art music have been ignored, and the tastes and feelings of the public about music have been distorted.

The educated man, then, eager to make music a part of his education, faces the problem of how to come to know the literature of great music: he can't read music—few professionals can; he can't perform it himself—this would be by far the best way, on no matter which level of expertness, but amateurism is unfortunately so little developed in this country that the music lover has to resort to other means. The radio will not furnish them for obvious reasons. Its repertoire of fine music is restricted to a small number of works which by their endless repetition have been made into instruments of advertising. The recording industry, of course, follows the same pattern. But besides this restriction, recordings are by their very nature inadequate to bring the nonprofessional listener into the proper contact with great music: they lack the dimension of immediateness and intensity necessary to provoke adequate receptive attitudes. I hold the fact that, *faute de mieux*, records are the chief means of communication with music literature and are largely responsible for the deterioration of listening habits.

The living performance still has the function of adequate presentation of great works of music. But in order to fulfill it, it has to be completely removed from the hedonism of the amusement industry and changes have to be made at both ends. The listener must be aroused to active intellectual and emotional participation. That can be done only by making the work speak directly to him. The performer must put himself behind the work, and all exhibitionistic attitudes which put him between the music and the listener must disappear. As long as audiences speak as they do of "Toscanini's Seventh Symphony," when they mean Beethoven's, or tell you that they liked "your music" so much, meaning that of the composers whose works you have performed, the situation is wrong. As long as the present system prevails it is clear that the changes will not occur within the music business.

I see an arrangement such as the one in which I have a part—that is, the appointment of musicians like the members of the Pro Arte Quartet here at the University of Wisconsin as artists in residence—as a promising and sorely needed opportunity to restore the true function of public musical performance and make it an essential instrument in the life of an educated man. By multiplying these arrangements the university can play again, as it has in earlier stages of history, an important role in the extension of musical culture.